Ad

"*MotherMorphosis* is a compassionate and humorous 'must-read' for mothers to be and mothers in the making."

Mark Victor Hansen, Co-creator, #1 New York Times best-selling series *Chicken Soup for the Soul®*, Co-author, *The One Minute Millionaire*

"*MotherMorphosis* is an exceptional book created to capture the personal nuances of evolving as a parent and the responsibilities that come with motherhood. This book shares a deeply profound perspective on the multifaceted and complex aspects of caring for children."

R. Scott Brooks, Book Evaluator, ***Writer's Digest***

"*MotherMorphosis* is essential for any new mom trying to figure out the complexities of motherhood. Ms. Poser tenderly touches on those issues mothers can so easily relate to: the loss of our independence—and our figures—and the overwhelming emotions women experience when raising a child."

Cynthia M. Allegrezza, Book Review Editor, ***Today's Parent***

"Caroline Poser is in the mix. It's like she's kept a travelogue of her journey into motherhood, keenly noting all the strange flora and fauna and dark corners for the rest of us to marvel at. And we do marvel, because even though motherhood is unique to each one of us, it's also a profoundly shared experience. Poser is brilliant at picking up a detail, dusting it off, and sharing it with us in essays that are ripe, funny, and full of truths."

Julie Tilsner, editor *Parenting Magazine,* author of three humor books, as well as the best-selling *29 & Counting: A Chick's Guide to Turning 30*

"I love this book. Caroline provides a unique and humorous perspective on motherhood at its best and worst. It's sure to help mothers retain their sanity and sense of humor during those hairy-scary child raising years that only seem funny when you look back at them after they are grown. Wish *MotherMorphosis* had been available when I was raising my two. Delightful!"

Sheila Gautreaux-Lee, Founder of "Spiritual DIVAs" and author of *Messages: Essays on a Spiritual Journey* and *Praying Through a Storm*

"There are various milestones by which we gauge our lives and having children is one of them. *MotherMorphosis* is a charming book that pays tribute to our struggles and sacrifices as we morph our way into motherhood. It's the Thank You card for all of us women who eat the 'burnt pork chop.'"

Tomi Tuel, author of *101 Things I Learned After My Divorce*

"In a way I spent the weekend with you - I just read your book and really enjoyed it! There are formula stains all over it as I did most of my reading while holding my baby."

Karen Bressler, CEO, AGAR Supply Company

"Caroline's honesty about motherhood at its best and worst moments is truly an inspiration. Her stories are so real, so honest…so refreshing."

Sandy Grason, best-selling author of *JOURNALUTION: Journaling to Awaken Your Inner Voice, Heal Your Life and Manifest Your Dreams.*

"In *MotherMorphosis*, Caroline gets it! She sees what we so often fail to see, the moments that make up parenting. The ones we can easily walk by if we're not careful. Plus, her sense of humor reminds us not to take ourselves too seriously. After all, we're here to love and laugh, aren't we?"

Jim Warda, author of *Where Are We Going So Fast?*

MotherMorphosis

Vignettes about the Transformation Into and Within Motherhood

Caroline B. Poser

Wyatt-MacKenzie Publishing, Inc.
DEADWOOD, OREGON

MotherMorphosis: Vignettes about the Transformation Into and Within Motherhood

by Caroline B. Poser

ISBN: 1-932279-26-1
Library of Congress Control Number: 2006924153

Published by The Mom-Writers Publishing Cooperative
Wyatt-MacKenzie Publishing, Inc., Deadwood, OR
www.WyMacPublishing.com (541) 964-3314

Cover photo by Sylvia Stagg-Giuliano www.Stagg-Giuliano.com

Requests for permission or further information should be addressed to:
Wyatt-MacKenzie Publishing, 15115 Highway 36, Deadwood, Oregon 97430

Printed in the United States of America

Dedication

For my sons

"Truly it is not easy to bring up a family," sighs Babar.

"But how nice the babies are! I wouldn't know how to get along without them any more."

Babar and His Children
Jean de Brunhoff

Foreword

If you are a mom-to-be, a new mom, or even a seasoned "veteran" mom, get ready to feel validated! In this precious book, Caroline tells the truth about becoming a mother. There are no frills here, nothing is dressed up to look like something it's not—all the stress, delight, tedium, wonder, fun, confusion, exhaustion, perfect moments and total chaos of creating a new family are laid out on the pages of these sweet stories for all of us to read…hungrily.

Although everyone's path is personal and unique, there is a universal quality to the inherent transformation of motherhood that shines through these stories. In the honest and thoughtful sharing of Caroline's life, I read my own story.

I, too, began my motherhood as a work-at-home mom. Twelve years later, with two fun and vivacious pre-teens, I spend my days working to balance the wants and needs of four very different and very busy people (my immediate family), as well as provide support of all kinds to my extended family—our moms and grandmas and aunts—while running my blooming (still home-based!) business, and striving to make time for self-care, friendship, and community.

Perhaps unsurprisingly, my company is called Balance For Life. I am a holistic health counselor and nutritionist in the business of supporting people in finding a healthy balance in their bodies, hearts, and minds. Mostly I work with women—again, unsurprisingly, mostly women who are mothers or moms-to-be.

I have a special place in my heart for those mother-clients whose children have already moved out of their birth homes and into the world. Perhaps I attract these women in particular because I need their wisdom as much as they need mine. They carry the secret treasures, not of success or even learning from failure, but of the direct experience of having walked the entire kids-at-home path already. Herein lies the real wisdom of motherhood: the living of it, all of it. And that is where we find the deepest gift of Caroline's book: in a rich offering of so many facets of the direct experience of her journey into motherhood.

This mothermorphosis is a messy business. The "balance" isn't always easy to see—certainly we don't often feel it. But our task is not to sort it all out and get everything "right". There is no "getting it right", no completion, no end to the story. Instead, with that first pink cross on the pregnancy test, our task is to dive in and live it—to feel and experience all the levels of the gift that we have been given. It's already right, right in the living.

I want to thank you, Caroline, for naming this profound transformation, for living so fully, bravely and with such humor into your mothermorphosis, for all you do for your boybies, and for sharing it with us all.

Jeannette Bessinger, HHC
Managing owner, Balance For Life, LLC
Ordained interfaith minister

Jeannette Bessinger, board certified holistic health counselor and owner of Balance For Life, LLC (www.balancelife.net), is the designer and lead facilitator of the innovative and successful *Enough Is Enough!* hospital-based lifestyle change/weight management program. She is a corporate nutritional consultant and serves on health and wellness councils for the Newport, Rhode Island public school system and Medical Home Initiative. She is also the co-author of *Is it Ready Yet? Simple Guidelines and Quick Healthy Recipes for Nourishing Busy Families.*

Introduction

All my life I knew I would have children.

When the time came, I took the birthing classes, studied the manuals diligently, and knew just what to expect during labor and delivery. But I was totally unprepared for everything that happened after I came home from the hospital.

Even though I'd read books, and talked with a lot of people—including my own mother—somehow I figured I would pretty much be the same old me, doing the same old stuff, just add kids. Boy was I wrong. And surprised! I barely remember the "same old me" and have no time to entertain any of the "same old stuff" anymore. My life changed overnight.

There just isn't any way to know in advance what it's going to be like, and I doubt that it would matter if you've taken care of other people's children (which I hadn't)—the operative words here being "other people's."

I felt so alone because most of my friends didn't want to talk about identity crises, juggling business responsibilities, their insecurities, or anything other than poop and "has he said 'dada' yet?" "But…" I wondered. "What about all the nitty-gritty hard parts of becoming a mother?" Surely I wasn't the only one who felt like I did!

So I started writing. And it came to pass that I wrote this book. Some of it is culled from my journals, some is derived from conversations with close friends, and much of it originated from conversations or experiences with my older two sons.

It evolved during the course of many years, written and compiled and rearranged in fits and starts—whenever I could squeeze out a few moments to myself (often in the middle of the night) and wherever I could jot down ideas ideally on my laptop, but often on whatever paper I could find).

Writing the book was my method of making sense of my intense period of personal, professional, emotional, spiritual, and of course, physical change. My MotherMorphosis®. Publishing it is my means of reaching out and touching other moms' lives, inspiring them, and connecting with them.

My ultimate goal is to honor and validate the delicate balancing act that mothers perform on a daily basis, the personal and professional sacrifices we make, and at the same time, the gratitude we feel for the tremendous gift we have received by having children.

My children are my "why." They are the reason I get up in the morning (sometimes too early)...the reason I go to work every day...the reason I do almost everything I do. They are my motivation, my inspiration, and my revelation: it is because of my children that I know the true love of God —I imagine the love I have for them is just like the love that God has—and my own parents have—for me. Thank you, God.

Contents

Remembering when *14*

Who am I now? *19*

And where did the day go? *21*

Mother's little helper *24*

Loser-dom *27*

Walking the tightrope *31*

Dressing for success *33*

Mark's baby *36*

Burnt pork chops *39*

Home sweet home improvement *41*

The waiting is the hardest part *45*

Becoming *47*

Living large *49*

Young (at heart, anyway) *51*

Keeping it together *53*

Softheartening *56*

My summer vacation *58*

The twilight zone of roles *60*

Style vs. comfort *63*

Witching hour *65*

Breaking the rules *67*

Drudgery *70*

Get out much? *71*

Not babysitting *74*

BrotherMorphosis *76*

My beauty regimen, then and now *81*

Weaning *84*

Moonlighting *87*

The Mommy-brain myth *93*

She's come undone *96*

Enrichment *99*

Holiday hangover *103*

The week from hell *105*

You must be a zombie *112*

Coffee juju *115*

Expectations *120*

The price of a shower *122*

The emergency room *126*

Diet and exercise *130*

Freelancing isn't working *134*

Why Mark takes vitamins *137*

The overdose *140*

Housewife by default *143*

Compliance insurance *146*

Dusting the blinds *150*

Doing the next right thing *154*

Thank you, God *157*

When the "next right thing"… isn't *162*

The natural mother onus *166*

My heroines *168*

My hopes for my sons *171*

MotherMorphosis

Vignettes about the Transformation Into and Within Motherhood

Remembering when

I was talking to an expecting mom who called me as a reference for our daycare the other day. It was winter and they were enrolling for the following school year.

I caught myself pontificating about how wonderful it is to be a mom and how it's the greatest thing you'll ever do, blah blah blah, etc. This woman was either just being polite, or she was evaluating exactly what kind of raving lunatic she was about to become: someone who "doesn't get out much" and is thrilled to talk to practically anyone over the age of two, because she let me go on and on…and on.

Daddy was away and I was in the midst of a really challenging week between sick kids, a work deadline, and three snowstorms. Really challenging.

Yet somehow I had conjured up feelings of wistfulness and nostalgia about pregnancy. I could put myself in this woman's shoes, in the days before the kids were actually here and before I really knew what motherhood is like—and couldn't possibly even imagine it—when the feeling of anticipation is palpable.

My mind wandered back to when I was first pregnant with Mark. I didn't really feel any different, but my period was a week late. Daddy brought home a pregnancy test and I just held the box and read every single word on it while I had my last cigarette. The knowledge of what-might-be was starting to sink in—and I stubbed the cigarette out halfway to the filter.

Minutes later, the test came back positive. I vowed to give up coffee, too. And every other naughty habit I had. All of a sudden there were tons of other pregnant women in the world. Where had they all been before?

I remembered scarcely being able to believe it could be true and being torn between wanting to keep the secret and wondering when it was okay to tell everyone ...relishing all the possibilities: was it a boy or a girl? ...who would it look like? ...how should we choose the name?

I remembered reading any book or article I could get my hands on about pregnancy and childbirth. I wanted to do everything "right."

I remembered worrying. Once my pregnancy became "official," I began to worry about *everything*. (It doesn't help that everyone has an opinion, offers it freely, and it's different than the last opinion I got!) When am I going to hear the heartbeat? When is the baby going to move? And later, am I feeling the baby move enough? And even later, "Baby, stop moving!" or "Baby, move off my bladder!"

I also worried about fatigue, weight gain, and would I be able to make it through the baby shower (never mind labor)? Is the baby "normal?" What if it's too big? Is my life ever going to be the same? What have I done? Was I keeping my stress level low enough? (Was I worrying too much?)

I remembered my debut in maternity clothes. It was a Sunday and as we walked to church I felt as awkward and self-conscious as I did the first day I wore a bra.

I remembered getting up in the middle of the night (after a Technicolor dream) to eat—even in my first trimester. Ice cream and cold steak. Tater tots. Candy. I was voraciously hungry ...utterly exhausted ...completely vibrant and alive. Sometimes all at once.

I remembered the rushing sound of the ocean in my ears. I imagined it was my circulatory system working overtime. Often I could see the pulse in my wrist. This must have been what made me feel so hot all the time. My body was like an oven, baking "the bun." I remembered that awesome feeling of butterfly wings inside my belly and later on, when I could feel through my own skin a knee, a shoulder, and the baby's head.

I remembered being emotional. I cried at least daily—every time there was a sappy show on like *Touched by an Angel.* I cried when I sampled a lullaby tape. I cried more than usual in church. I cried on the way to the doctor appointments. I cried one morning when there was a segment on a talk show about adopted kids getting reunited with their birth parents. I cried when I saw road kill. I cried while I was trying to pick out greeting cards. I cried while reading good news stories in the newspaper. And I *always* cried during *A Baby Story* on Lifetime TV—*especially* when they showed the baby being born and I heard its first cry. I remembered crying tears of joy, gratitude, pain (physical), farewell (to my old self), and guilt (during my second pregnancy when Mark was no longer going to be my one and only)—and the whole range of emotions was magnified.

I remembered when we were expecting Mark and Daddy made a comment to the effect of "this may be our last weekend alone." And he was right. It was. Mark was born the following Thursday. He was two weeks early.

Then I thought about all the delightful (and sometimes less delightful) aspects of newborns...how small and wiggly and velvety and noisy they are—grunting, squeaking, squealing, and snorting in addition to crying ...so much crying! ...and how sometimes I would just watch them sleep and see the whole repertoire of human expression pass across their faces, as if they were being programmed for life.

When I was pregnant with Mark, I was lucky enough to be expecting at the same time as one of my good friends from college. We were both having our first children, we both had similar careers, and we were due within a week of each other. We compared notes the entire time (via email since we live on opposite coasts). Mark came early, and her son came late, and I remember waiting on the edge of my seat (pretty much how all new mothers have to sit) for *two whole weeks* until we could continue our daily reality checks.

One thing I *hadn't* concerned myself about while I was pregnant with Mark was figuring out childcare. (It no doubt would have been just one more thing to worry about.) Part of the rosy picture of motherhood I had painted in my mind, without fully being able to comprehend what having a baby was like, was (since I work at home) that I would be able to work while the baby slept. Well, I tried that, and it *just* didn't work.

"What were you thinking?" one of the teachers at the recent daycare open house had asked me.

She had referred to me as a "veteran" to another mom, and then asked how old my kids were when they started at the daycare. (I certainly didn't feel like a veteran—though I suppose I was after almost two years of experience—considering there was a time when I couldn't even imagine surviving boot camp.) I told her Baby Chase was nearly eight weeks but Mark was seven months, and then I confessed the part about how I thought I could work around his nap schedule. In reply to her question, I told her, "I *wasn't* thinking. I had no idea the amount of work having a baby entailed."

Because I went so long without help the first time around, I am extremely appreciative of the value of our daycare (a.k.a. "school," depending upon with whom I'm speaking), which is why I was having the conversation with the woman on the phone to begin with.

It was just what I needed at that particular point in time. It helped me remember how truly lucky I am. Because for all the times I am stretched to the limits of patience, fatigue, and worry because of my children—or in the midst of a "really challenging" week—having them is the most blessed and enriching thing I have ever done.

Who am I now?

I could barely remember who I was before I had this baby, yet at the same time, when people called me "Mommy" I did a double take. "Oh, yeah… that's right. That's *me*!"

I did have *some* experience with kids, because Daddy came with three medium-sized ones. However, I never spent much time with babies before I had one. Indeed, my own was the first newborn I had ever held.

I was overwhelmed by the transformation I had not only gone through by giving birth, but also was going through by learning to become a mother. I was overwhelmed by being on call 24x7. I was overwhelmed because I felt like I couldn't do anything right.

My confidence washed in and out like the tide. I wished I could have brought a nurse home from the hospital, too, because I had no one to tell me what to do or when to do it (except a tiny tyrant who screamed until I got it right). There was so much conflicting advice. And just the smallest comment or allusion could make me doubt myself.

"Let him cry it out."
"Don't feed him whenever he wants."
"You have to get him on a schedule." (He *was* on a schedule—his.)
"Don't give him a pacifier."
"Don't let him suck his thumb"
"You're *still* breastfeeding?" (This came at six and eight weeks from different people.)

I clung desperately to my old self—career-oriented and competent businesswoman—because I was sure about who that person was.

Yet, it was so hard to keep up with my "normal" work schedule, because there was just so much more to do on the home front. This included keeping track of all the new and unfamiliar accessories and furnishings such as binkies, blankies, the bouncy seat, and the Diaper Genie. There were thank-you notes to write, rolls and rolls and rolls of film to be developed (and then pictures to sort), laundry to wash, fold, and put away, and then jungle detritus to clean up—dead remnants of all the once-beautiful and often exotic flower arrangements I brought home from the hospital that had dropped all over the tables and floor as they wilted and died (more likely as a result of my forgetting to water them than of age). And then—of course—everything took a back seat to *The Baby*. When he cried, it was clear what my priorities must be. I put on my Mommy hat.

Sometimes I felt like I stepped into someone else's life.

And where did the day go?

No amount of reading or talking to family or friends could have prepared me for becoming a mother—even though I thought I had learned to be a pretty good listener. You just don't know what you don't know.

I never believed I would spend the whole day being so busy that I wouldn't even think about what time it was until it started to get dark out. I'd wonder, "Where did the time go? What did I do all day?"

I had heard the joke about the man who comes home to find the house and yard a God-awful mess and the kids in dirty pajamas and his wife on the couch with a bag of chips and the latest suspense novel and there's no sign of dinner on the table. When he asks her, "Honey, what *happened*?" she says, "Well, darling, you know all those times you come home and ask me what in the world did I do all day? Well, today I didn't do it."

On the flipside, I had also heard stories about the proverbial "supermom" who *could* do it all…bring home the bacon, *and* cook it, while balancing her baby on her hip as well as being a smart, savvy, sophisticated wife.

Uh huh.

In the beginning, most days I was able to get dressed. (This might include taking a shower if I was *really* lucky.) Getting dressed meant that I managed to put on one pair or another of black leggings and a baggy shirt. Hardly a fashion statement, but my only alternative was maternity clothes and I really didn't want to wear them anymore.

So, where *did* the day go?

Well, for starters, even the little bit of sleep I could get during the night was likely to come to a screeching halt at 5:00 a.m. or sometimes as early as 4:00 with that little wailing voice that had become oh-so-familiar and compelling. Our day would begin.

I learned that feeding a newborn is not a simple matter. It takes time. And then it takes more time to produce a bubble. If he didn't burp, he would cry in half an hour when the un-erupted bubble started to irritate him. And then hopefully he wouldn't get the hiccups because the only thing that cures newborn hiccups is swallowing, and the only way he could swallow was by nursing. Then he might swallow more air, which would necessitate being burped again. (I have been told that hiccups bother the mom more than the baby, but I am not completely convinced.)

Meanwhile, what goes in must come out, so he needed to have his diaper changed. But I didn't necessarily want to do it after the feeding, because I might "push his baby button"—inadvertently compress his stomach as I lifted his bottom up—which could cause him to spit up, which might require more feeding, and maybe new clothes, too.

Ideally, I would want to change his pants before nursing, but if he woke up hungry, he would want to eat right away. Thus, I would have to hear him cry (and so would others in the house), if we did the pre-meal change. That was not optimal when it happened in the middle of the night; so, I learned to change him mid-feeding. A lot of times, as soon as I got his fresh diaper on he would poop, which meant starting all over...again.
Now, if a baby eats every two hours, that means from start time to start time (just like how you count contractions,

isn't that something?). Theoretically, I could be busy with baby care for a whole hour and then I might get an hour off while he was napping. Everyone says that you should nap when the baby naps. But if you do this, when do you eat or go to the bathroom? (Never *mind* taking care of the house or working). And in the beginning this is hard, because every time you go to the bathroom it is a major ordeal, the details of which I will spare you.

So, as I *now* know, basic newborn care takes up most—if not all—of one's time. And feeding-burping-changing can happen at any time during a given 24-hour period: a newborn does not discriminate and certainly doesn't care whether the rest of the family usually sleeps when it's dark out.

Prior to gaining this knowledge, if anyone had told me that I would have a hard time getting to the mailbox on any given day, I would have laughed. "No way, not me!" Especially since our mailbox was about ten steps from the front door.

Mother's little helper

My very pregnant friend, who has two cats, asked me how our cats took to Mark when I brought him home from the hospital.

I thought about the early days when just as I would get settled in to nurse him, Teensy, our little gray girlcat, would do something naughty, like jump up on the bureau and either skid into something or prance around, both of which would have the same effect of knocking over the lamp, my watch or earrings, Mark's shoes, clean laundry, or a stack of books—whatever was on it.

Many things that were once on the bureau ended up on the floor or behind the bureau, including my water bottle. "Arghhhhhhh! I forgot to screw the cap on all the way again!" I would lament, and once more, I had a puddle to clean up.

Sometimes she wanted to play a game of let's-climb-up-Mommy's-legs-to-see-what-she's-doing-with-that-baby-in-her-lap (as if I could possibly be doing anything new and different). Having failed to dress for the occasion (as I was wearing those thin black leggings), I ended up with claw holes in my leg before I nudged—okay, swatted—her off.

Often I had to prod her off the changing table where she had perched to supervise what was going on. She would chirp and twitter, "Notice me, notice me—oh don't forget about me!"

"Believe you me, Teensy, I see you and I hear you!"

I had no one to blame but myself, really. I created this monster. When Mark was born, Daddy brought home his little newborn hat from the hospital to let the cats get used to his smell, like they suggested in our prenatal classes. I guess that went over like a lead balloon, because when we brought Mark home, Teensy wanted no part of him. In fact she hissed and sidestepped and turned kind of nasty—she behaved like a jealous toddler.

(Our boycat, T-Bone, gave us all a wide berth; we had adopted him from a shelter and on the documentation that came with him, his previous owners said they had a new baby who was "allergic" to cats. T-Bone has it pretty good at our house and might not have wanted to take any chances.)

Fearful that she was going to steal his breath in the night, I decided to encourage a friendship between Teensy and Mark. Whenever I fed Mark, I would give Teensy some cat treats. Well, like Pavlov's dogs, she came to associate feeding-the-baby with treats. Or maybe she is a little smarter than Pavlov's dogs. I think she knew that if Mark was fussing or crying, Mommy went to him. Apparently babies didn't fuss or cry enough on their own for her taste, because it seemed that she even figured out how to wake him up. I never quite caught her doing it, but sometimes I was so quick to respond to Mark's cries that I arrived in time to see her slinking away with that telltale sideways glance—the guilty look (anthropomorphism be damned)—before she darted back around behind me and escorted me in to Mark's room, good Samaritan that she is.

Or if I was a little slower on the draw, she would seek me out and sashay across my keyboard, or start scratching the furniture, or get in the middle of whatever I might be doing. "Mommy, Mommy, Baby's crying!"

"Thanks, Teensy. What a good little helper!"

I wound up telling my friend, "You might notice some new and unusual behavior. The changes in your household will affect your cats, too…but, *whatever* you do, don't start giving them treats!"

Loser-dom

Sometimes I feel like such a loser parent.

It can be the smallest thing that triggers this feeling—ranging from the time I brought Mark in for his two-week check up and bonked his head on the scale when I laid him down in it to his teacher's friendly suggestion to "mix up" his lunch choices to fellow shoppers' comments (or even just double-takes) about the latest public meltdown…or the times I run into people I know and I have some eclectic combination of clothes on. Add to this that on some occasions, I have not showered yet and still have the same clothes on that I slept in and/or that I may have even worn the day before. (It seems like I always run into someone I know on these days. I cringe and shudder.)

Sometimes I find myself talking and I just can't stop. The people on the other side of the counter of the bank, post office, and other stores I frequent probably think I'm nuts. Even I think I'm nuts sometimes as I walk out the door. I no doubt have cabin fever. After being in the house most of the day, it's just nice to talk to another adult. I catch myself making unnecessary conversation on the phone, too. Routine calls to the doctor's office or to the electric company take on new significance.

Occasionally I dwell on the fact that I seem to be the only mom at daycare and possibly church—and maybe even this whole town—without a seven-passenger vehicle. Okay, so I exaggerate. There are a couple of other parents who pull up at daycare in sedans or station wagons, and I think there is even one hatchback. (God only knows how you get a car seat in and out of that without breaking your back.) But these families' *other* vehicles are probably SUVs or vans! (At the playground recently, I counted 11 vehicles and *all* of them were minivans or SUVs except for one Volvo station wagon…and my mid-sized Nissan sedan.)

Once, not long after Mark was first born, I was going to take him out for a walk and to the supermarket (which is not much farther away than the mailbox). I *finally* figured out how to put the baby-wearing-carrier-device together, but by then it was time to nurse him, and of course I had to change him first (the philosophy to which I ascribed at the time—now, if the diaper's not poopy or close to capacity, I'm not changing it!), and then I was concerned that if I jostled him around, he would throw up. When we were finally ready to go, I realized that his snowsuit didn't even have legs (it was just one of those bunting thingies) so I couldn't even *use* the carrier. It was supposed to convert to a sling, too, but when I tried that, he was all folded up on himself. It sure didn't look too comfortable. I felt like a failure.

But one of the most absolutely awful, worst embarrassing times was early on when I had met another new mother who lived a couple of blocks away, so we made plans to go for a walk together. I remember the elaborate planning that went into this outing—getting the timing just right so that Mark wouldn't need to eat or have a diaper change while we were out. (And I courteously called her right before I left the house so she could perform similar preparatory rituals to mine at her house. Though, come to find out, she was so with-it that she probably had a fully-stocked diaper bag packed and ready to go at the drop of a hat.)

Amongst all the baby hand-me-downs I'd received were two umbrella strollers. One had no canopy, however it did have a basket and pretty good wheels—but without shade, we couldn't go out on sunny days. Since it was winter, if it wasn't sunny, it wasn't really a good day to go out anyway. The other had a canopy but awful wheels and no basket, so it was useless to take shopping—it was next to impossible to maneuver in the aisles. I felt oafish enough as it was, and adding this stroller, whose wheels couldn't have been parallel, often caused me to stagger clumsily, barely avoiding displays or other shoppers. And, like all umbrella strollers, the handles were too low (picture Quasimodo after having a few too many). But since we weren't going shopping, and it was a sunny day, this is the stroller I selected.

So I showed up at my neighbor's house and she had her baby tucked in neatly under some sort of fleecy thing that fit right over the car seat that fit right into the stroller, in such a way that she could gaze adoringly at him. Her stroller had a drink holder and a place to stash things built into the handle, too.

Our mission: to walk to the oil company to pay her bill. So, it figures, I got to parade my inadequacy all through downtown (as well as at the oil company where I know everyone in the front office so of course we got to show off our babies, and again, my maternal shortcomings). It felt like one of those dreams you have where you're at school and you realize there's a final exam that day...that you didn't prepare for ...and there are only five minutes left...and you're naked... and you have to pee...and you can't run fast enough...and you're about to fall off a cliff. But this wasn't a dream—it was *real!*

I remember trying so hard to control the stroller, so that I didn't ram it into my neighbor's "travel system." The tension in my arms from trying to act nonchalant as I forced this little stroller onto the straight and narrow was quite tiring.

Compounding my misery as I recount this episode is the fact that I found out shortly after our walk that you are not supposed to use umbrella strollers with babies who cannot sit up unassisted. When I learned this, mortification washed over me anew.

Thankfully, over time, I have been able to either lighten up about these events or simply leave them in the past. And the stroller story does have a happy ending—as soon as I could, I began my quest for the "right" stroller. I looked at catalogs, perused websites, and studied other friends' choices. At last I was ready to go to the store.

But even though Mark and I had to stop at a church parking lot to nurse on the way to the store, he wanted to nurse *again* before I was done shopping. Since I did not want to give up on my mission, especially because I already had some things in the shopping cart, I did the only thing I could—I nursed him as I continued shopping.

A very pregnant woman approached me in awe and said, "Wow—I can't believe you can do that *and* shop at the same time …I hope I will be able to be so natural when the time comes."

Flattered, I replied, "Well, you do whatever you have to do…I am sure you'll do just fine!"

My confidence shored up, I went on to scope out the stroller selection. I was elated when I realized that the stroller I liked actually fit together with the car seat that Daddy had picked out so that I was no longer a loser—I had my own travel system.

Walking the tightrope

Sometimes there is a fine line between having it all together and completely losing it.

I am recalling one time that I chit-chatted too long with our babysitter when she came to pick up Mark. And then, just as I was rushing to get ready to leave for a client meeting, a truck arrived with two pallets of stones that Daddy had ordered. I had taken down the signs he posted to instruct the driver where to dump them, because we had already received two pallets earlier that morning, and I figured that was it.

While I was obsessing about whether or not the truck driver was going to drop the stones in the right place, as precisely specified by Daddy, I was trying to change my clothes and make a sandwich to eat en route to the client. And then I noticed that I had accidentally left the front door ajar. My stomach dropped.

T-Bone had been hit by a car the week before, and even though when I took him to the vet to get checked out, he was mostly fine, he was *not* supposed to go outside.

All I could think about as I started darting around the house calling, "Kitty, here kitty, where are you…T-Bone…Kitty, kitty, KITTY (@$^*& cat!)" was having to call my client and make up some excuse for being late. The truth would be too silly in this case. And really, there is no excuse for being late to a client meeting. *And I was already running late!*

It turned out that T-Bone had not even noticed the open

door. He was snoozing under the bed. What a relief. As I gathered the remainder of my wits, I prayed that the stone delivery truck would be gone so I could leave the driveway. It was.

So, I was finally on my way. I meandered through the back roads of my quaint town, and got held up by "downtown" lunchtime traffic. Once I got to the highway, there were only 20 minutes to get to the client's office, which was probably about 20 not-all-highway miles away. I drove 80 m.p.h., alternately praying and eating my sandwich. I told myself if it got to be ten minutes of the hour and I was still not within range, I would call. But when my dashboard clock read 12:50, I couldn't bring myself to call. I cursed the guy in front of me who I was tailgaiting when he let someone out of a parking lot before he turned in. Finally, I pulled in to the office complex parking lot with two minutes to spare.

I parked in the less-remote customer parking section of the vast lot (I'm kind of a customer, right?) and strode quickly to the entrance, almost panting, trying to think cool thoughts for a humid August day. As I approached the front door, I breathed deeply and slowed my pace…assuming the semblance of the laid-back.

The design team was there waiting. They had signed me in.

"Thank you very much, nice to see you," and other pleasantries were exchanged, and I clipped on my "Visitor" badge just as the client walked around the corner to escort us to the conference room for our meeting. Everything was cool, but I wondered if anyone could tell that only moments before I was on the verge of completely losing it.

Dressing for success

My dilemma was such that I had a client meeting, but seemingly nothing to wear. I couldn't fit into any of my old clothes and I *really* didn't want to wear maternity clothes anymore. And anyway, I had already given the bulk of them back to my friend, who lent them to me to begin with…she was pregnant again.

I already wore my one decent outfit—flowing patterned pants and an off-white, long (maternity) shirt—at a meeting earlier that week. I could wear it again, but this meeting would be attended by the same design team as the previous meeting. Not that I really thought the *male* half of the design team would notice…he would probably wear the same blue suit, maybe change his tie. But what if he *did* notice? What if he had a Felix Unger side to his personality and thought about those things? *Everyone* knows you can't wear the same outfit twice in a row (even though I do it all the time at home if it doesn't have noticeable food or spit up on it)—we're not in college anymore.

So, the day before the meeting, I parked Mark in front of a video in my bedroom and proceeded to try on clothes. Everything revolved around one particular pair of off-white shoes, because I didn't want to wear dark shoes and—God forbid—hose (I had only worn hose twice in the previous year and a half—at my wedding and on the airplane to Mexico when I was pregnant because I was told doing so would keep my ankles and feet from swelling. But what it really did was make my ankles and feet *and* legs look like sausage links).

I didn't have a huge shoe wardrobe because not many of my pre-pregnancy shoes fit, other than flip-flops or slippers. (I've actually left the house and got into the car wearing slippers. Sure, they go with my outfit, but imagine walking into a client office wearing them!)

The shoes went with two pairs of pants—one of which I wore the other day and one of which I wore to the client meeting prior (sigh…again, with the same designers), and a skirt. But this skirt billowed out around my hips, so it was definitely not my first choice. Though, wait, could I wear it with the maternity shirt I wore the other day…nope, that didn't look too good. Tentlike.

I had two pairs of maternity Capri pants, but I would have to wear a long shirt to cover the stretch panel. That same shirt again …? But as I mentioned, it was off-white, and the Capri pants were either tan or black. Boring. I had a few other longer tank top numbers…one without a collar but with flattering stripes…no, my "bra overhang" (any flesh that gets squeezed out of your bra that could not possibly be considered cleavage) is unsightly. Could I layer this button-down thingy over it like a twin set…no, the white part showed through and looked like an undergarment. Strike that idea. And anyway, I think Capri pants might just be too casual.

I had a couple of dresses, but one was *way* too tight across the bust (imagine!) and the other was too tight across the belly. That one was kind of too feminine anyway. This was a *business* meeting. I needed to remain somewhat gender neutral.

I found a knit shirt/skirt combo in the back of the closet. The top was waaaaay too tight, but the skirt might work with that maternity shirt hmmmm….this looked okay....except, I just wasn't sure above the knee was okay without panty hose.

Maybe I should try on that green linen dress again...no, it's *still* too tight. Can't have those buttons coming undone.

Flowery shirt? Needed ironing. I don't iron. Forget that idea.

I was practically in tears as I rejected and subsequently flung what seemed like half my closet onto the bed. Then I realized Mark was watching *me*—not his video—with big round eyes. I felt ridiculous.

I decided to wear those flowing patterned pants and the off-white maternity shirt after all. And though it took me half an hour to get right back where I started, at least I knew I had made the right choice—because it was the *only* choice!

Mark's baby

I was in Toys R Us one day to buy a baby shower gift for a friend. That was my excuse for being there anyway. Sure, I also needed to stock up on the store-brand diapers for Mark. But, probably because I was pregnant, all of a sudden my nesting instinct kicked into overdrive.

I decided I would buy some things for Baby-on-the-way, like a "Soothing Sounds" teddy bear (yes, it makes womb noises and I had one for Mark so I *had* to get a similar one for the new baby), and a soft photo album (*just* like Mark's—I want to treat both kids equally, after all), as well as an additional monitor, since Mark and the baby would have separate rooms.

So, since I had shifted into high-gear shopping, I decided that day was a good time to buy some things that I had on my wish list for Mark for a while, too, like pint-sized furniture. I got him a couch, chair, and ottoman. He loved the ones at daycare, and I *did* need to usurp (for its original purpose) his Boppy nursing pillow, which he had been using as a seat for several months. I also found a set of number and letter sponge bathtub toys (the reasoning here was that bathtime had been very difficult in recent days and hopefully this would add the impetus needed to actually bathe). And I included a couple of board books about ABCs and shapes, and—why not?—an Elmo video about babies and puppies, so I could have spare presents on-hand in case visitors brought Baby a gift but not Mark. Then, last but not least, I went on the hunt for a doll. The logic behind this was to get Mark used to the idea of having another "baby" around.

Finding just the right doll was a lot harder than I thought. First of all, most of the dolls are for kids ages three and above. Mark was just 15 months at that time. And most of them are targeted towards girls, which is obvious by the marketing message on the package: "her first doll," "Little Mommy" and the like. And I didn't want one with lots of bells and whistles—my main goal was to find a small, inexpensive doll whose eyes closed when it was put to rest. I did not want one that talked or cried or could be comforted by putting a pacifier in its mouth (I didn't want to teach Mark that to quiet a baby you plug its mouth...and I also didn't want to give him any ideas about pacifiers—he hadn't used them since he was about four months old). I did not want a super-sized baby or a character baby (Kewpie or Cabbage Patch). I just wanted a simple, generic baby.

As I was wandering up and down the aisles, I realized I was starting to lose my focus. I found myself wallowing in remorse for even *having* another baby. I (kind of) remember how I felt when my brother arrived on the scene...I was almost three. I am not sure if I specifically remember, or if I can identify with the love-hate feelings that are expressed so clearly on my pouting face and by my pushing-him-aside body language in early photos of my brother and me. And as I projected these feelings onto Mark, my heart began breaking for him.

The poor little guy would be only 17 months old (give or take), depending on when the baby arrived. How was I going to explain to him that he—my one-and-only—would no longer be the only one? That the new baby was ours to keep and would be here to stay?

I had a hard time pushing the guilt aside, even though my mom had reminded me that it is important for children to know how to fit into their family, neighborhood, and society as a whole. Another thing I heard was the best gift you can give to your child is a sibling. And I also recalled a very bittersweet tidbit someone had shared, "Don't worry—he won't even remember the time before the baby is born." And my eyes welled up with tears. So that meant all the special times we shared would be mine and mine alone to recollect? (Gee, thanks.) Surely they would be imprinted somewhere in his psyche, wouldn't they?

I wound up choosing a doll that had pink clothes, because it was the only Caucasian one I liked. It came with a rubber ducky and a bottle (it was a "drink-and-wet" doll). I thought, "Great…more reinforcement for bathing, and maybe we can learn something about going potty."

When I presented Mark with the doll, he exclaimed, "Ay-mee, mah AY-mee! Mama! AY-MEE! Yay yay YAY!" and took to her like a long-lost friend. "Hmmmm…" I thought. "I hope he greets his new sibling with the same enthusiasm." (I later found out that Mark's babysitter's daughter had the exact same doll and had named her Amy.)

Burnt pork chops

"You already had your first burnt pork chop," my friend said as we were sitting around the table at our monthly investment club meeting.

"Huh?" a few of us did double takes. Two of us were pregnant at the time and we had been commiserating over our sciatica and charley horses.

My friend continued, "As a kid I wondered why my mother always took the crumbs of the pie, had the biggest hole in the soles of her shoes, saved the cream off the top of the milk bottle for someone else...and if a pork chop was burnt, it had her name on it. I know, after sacrificing for my family, that it's just what mothers do. And, listening to you girls talk, I just now realized how *soon* mothers begin to sacrifice, before the baby is even born."

This friend is from a different generation, so the milk-bottle analogy is a little irrelevant to me. I get her drift, though. I remember things like my mom gnawing on chicken leg bones (we never had anything like boneless breasts when I was a kid) after my brother and I had finished with them. She said she *liked* the cartilage and marrow! Yuck! And "helping" us with our ice cream cones so she didn't have to spend money on her own. These were my mom's burnt pork chops.

Furthermore, I heard stories about when my mom was growing up and they used to hand paint baby food tin cans for their Christmas tree ornaments (baby food in tin cans is also irrelevant...I never knew it came in anything besides little glass jars). My grandparents still had some of these ornaments when I was growing up, and I thought they were cool. My mom told me my grandmother was always embarrassed about them, as she was of the army surplus vehicle that was their family car. These were my grandmother's burnt pork chops.

So, the question is, what are *my* burnt pork chops, aside from sciatica and charley horses? I could tick off things like the fact that I don't have time to sleep any more and the house is usually a mess. But what mom of little kids doesn't have these problems? I never seem to have the right stroller for the occasion—figuratively speaking—and I am practically the only mom I know who doesn't have some sort of oversized vehicle. But these aren't showstoppers, either.

Perhaps my biggest burnt pork chops to date are the loss of my "girlish" figure and the fact that my career is in neutral. But big deal about these things, too. It won't be this way forever.

I think the point my friend was trying to make is that all moms have burnt pork chops and it's just a known fact. And we eat them because, in the grand scheme of things, what are a few burnt pork chops compared to the blessing of having children?

Home sweet home improvement

I was seven-plus months pregnant with Baby Chase and people were telling me "get your rest now; you won't get any after the baby is born." As if I didn't know that—I already had one baby! And anyway, when was I supposed to get this rest? As I mentioned, *I already had one baby* (and my work and a home improvement project I was managing).

One day, Mark slept all the way until 5:30 a.m., which was great (better than 4:30 anyway!). I got up with him and we did our normal morning routine of changing his diaper and getting a bottle and playing with toys and watching Elmo's World on Sesame Street.

Daddy also got up early to paint the trim boards for our couldn't-be-finished-soon-enough basement room. (He was job sharing the carpenter portion of our renovation with a friend who actually is a carpenter.) He came up to take a shower and when he was done it was my turn. Thank *God* I got to start my day with a shower. It always makes me feel like I have something accomplished. (I checked my email while I was "free," too.)

Then on the way out the door at 7:30ish, Daddy asked me to have the excavators call him as soon as they arrived. (They were usually there *by* 7:30, but Daddy just couldn't delay his departure any longer in case he got stuck in commuter traffic). They showed up at 8:30 or so, and that meant I spent about an hour peeking out the window so I could intercept them before they started working. I didn't want to have to wave them off their heavy equipment. But as soon as I saw their truck and went out to find them, I couldn't. I wound up leaving a note on their windshield, which, if I had done this in the first place would have spared me the hour of Kravitzing.

At 8:45 I decided I better move my car because I didn't want to get blocked in by the driveway work. As I was about to go out the door, there was the traveling salesperson who was trying for the third time to talk to me (I had blown her off the first two times), about to ring the bell.

She was a seemingly nice college student from Nebraska who was trying to sell me early learning books. I listened to her spiel, but told her that my son needed something earlier than what she had. Daddy had admonished me to watch out for these door-to-door out-of-staters, because they are really just casing the joint. So I was paranoid the whole time and wound up asking her just as many questions as she asked me.

Right after she left, I realized, "Oh my gosh—Mark's babysitter will be here any minute!" She came and together we finished getting Mark dressed before she took him away. I think it was library day.

Shortly after, our electrician showed up. I had prepared a list of questions for him because I was hoping to get the electrical inspection done that day, so we could finish the walls. If it wasn't for this electrician, who was somewhat fatherly, I think I would have been completely overwhelmed by this whole project. He was the one who clued me in to the politics of the building department and all the various inspections and the order of events that would need to occur to finish our basement. And through this whole experience, I learned why a general contractor gets paid a percentage of the job, and I will not engage in such an extravaganza so lightheartedly again.

Our carpenter came but couldn't do much but patch a few holes and saw some boards. He was also waiting for the electrical inspector, who came just as the electrician was finishing. He signed off (thank God) and then the electrician and I settled our current bill and discussed future outside work.

I checked in with myself again via e-mail, made some phone calls, dealt with a few church things, then realized it was almost 11:00. I needed to get some batteries and also light bulbs for the new basement fixtures. I thought about doing this during the noon hour, but that time period was pretty booked. Among other things, I had to drop T-Bone off for an ultrasound—the vet suspected he might have a liver problem.

I ran out to the hardware store and got back just in time to collect T and be on my way to his doctor (I never want to arrive at the vet's early...it's really no fun waiting around with a cat or two in a cardboard box), but he was not where he was when I left—so much for "perfect timing."

I think he knew. He was hiding. I was looking all over the house and getting annoyed because I had x amount of things I planned to accomplish before my 1:30 lunch date! I started stomping around and calling "Kitty...*Kitty*, ***Kitty***, **KITTY**!!!" I finally found him hiding under a chair and just about busted a gut trying to haul him out. Seriously, something pulled in my abdomen, which made walking very difficult, and I was absolutely certain I had undone everything the chiropractor did the day before.

T was silent the whole way to the vet. I felt guilty. I hobbled in and dropped him off. Then I headed to the carpet place in the next town over so I could settle with them and redeem my coupon for $100 off the rug that was being installed the next day. When I finished, I was cutting it close, but I went to the supermarket to get some supplies for lunch and dinner (I knew as long as I didn't wind up getting into a conversation with anyone, I could make it) and then headed over to pick up Mark. I made it home at 1:25ish, and the plumber was there...with the water turned off.

I checked in with him and then went out to talk to the excavators, to make sure they got my note. My lunch date arrived with a yummy salad. She was on a diet but I was not, so I had some cheese and crackers with the salad. I was *starving*. Thank God I had the batteries to put in Mark's favorite Elmo toy...he amused himself for so long I was actually able to eat and have a conversation. Eventually he wanted to join us (even though he'd had lunch at his babysitter's). So I fed him cheese, crackers, and applesauce until it became apparent that what he really needed was a nap. I don't know how he did it, but he slept through all the noise of the trucks and tractors in our yard, something I would not be able to do.

After I put Mark to bed, I decided to make cookies while my friend knitted and we talked. The cookies were for Daddy to take to work (I made something every Thursday for him to bring in on Friday) and also for him to share with his young friend from church who he was helping get confirmed, and heck ... while I'm at it, why not make them for the workers, too? I wound up making nine trays of cookies when all was said and done.

I sat with my friend on the couch briefly and we looked at baby catalogs. Then she had to go. I walked her out and then went back in to call the vet. I could pick T-Bone up any time before six. "Good," I thought. "Plenty of time for Mark to finish his nap, and I would have time to check in with myself again" (i.e., my paying work).

I wondered again when it was, exactly, that I was supposed to rest.

The waiting is the hardest part

At my 38-week checkup when I was pregnant with Baby Chase, my doctor said, "You're measuring big. I think you should have an ultrasound" (which would be the first of that pregnancy).

"Finally, medical opinion agreed with everyone else!" I thought.

For weeks I had been asking my doctor if I was in the "*range* of normal" (he's rather noncommittal so I didn't want to put too much pressure on him), because friends and acquaintances—and even complete strangers—were constantly making comments about my size: "Are you having twins?" or "Are you *sure* about your due date?" (As *if* I would discuss my menstrual cycle or the moment of conception with any of them!)

I didn't ever remember a summer starting off so hot, and it wasn't even officially summer yet. But we were having 90-degree-plus days. I didn't even want to leave my house, but life had to go on. People in my supermarket and post office and at our town's Memorial Day parade were surprised to see me still walking around, often chasing after Mark, who was a toddler at the time.

Mark was born in February. I do not remember feeling as uncomfortable with him, and he was a big baby, too (approaching 10 pounds.). The only thing that made me miserable at the end of that pregnancy was the dentist visit I had scheduled. (One's gums tend to get very sensitive during pregnancy.)
But this time around, besides the heat bothering me, I could

barely sleep at night. The weight of my huge belly pulled my spine out of alignment, which pulled on my leg muscles, which in turn pulled on my nerves. I was often rudely awakened by sciatica, foot cramps, or worse: charley horses, for which the only cure seemed to be jumping out of bed and hobbling around until they subsided. I had tried stretching, but that was a catch-22—in order to stretch one muscle group, the opposing muscle group contracted—so in effect, I was simply relocating the charley horse.

My chiropractor's table dropped down in the middle to adapt for pregnant women. As time went on she had to add a roll to raise my hips to make even more belly room. At my last visit she had to wrap two towels around the roll. I didn't schedule an appointment for the following week because a) I hoped to have the baby by then and b) was not sure I'd fit on the table if I didn't.

The advice you get at the end of your pregnancy is to rest and eat right. Ahem. I had no room left in my abdominal cavity for my stomach (or any other organ) let alone the food that would go in it! Why, if this baby truly was a more-than-ten-pounder as the doctor suspected, hadn't it been born yet? Certainly he *must* be ready. *I* sure was!

Becoming

Labor. I need to mention this because it is the actual turning point of one's "becoming." But I won't go into any detail about my experiences because I don't want to predispose anyone to what labor is like. Everyone is different, every baby is different, and every labor is different.

It's true what people say about forgetting ("how quickly we…" and I guess that is why many of us have more than one child). I thought I would *always* remember the milestones and statistics of pregnancy. However, when I was pregnant with Baby Chase, I had a hard time answering when my doctor asked me how long my first labor was. Because when do you start counting? My body was getting ready for weeks, it seemed. And my doctor is a man so he's certainly not going to be able to empathize with me about the nuances of every sign and symptom.

I hadn't bothered with the refresher birthing classes the second time around, but I did wind up being glad I had saved my coursebooks, because at the end of my pregnancy, I was looking up what the signs of labor were. (Although a C-section was scheduled, I went into labor the day before.) I learned that there's no set order of events, either, because it was different each time I labored.

I abhor it when people tell "labor horror stories"—trying to outdo each other—especially to a mom who is pregnant with her first baby. For me, it was daunting enough to be expecting… and I could only imagine and project what labor *might* be like… and some of my friends—or even acquaintances—had so generously shared their stories, or exchanged knowing looks with each other at my baby shower... and then when it got down to the wire where I was very uncomfortable and I wanted to have the baby, then again I *didn't* want to have it yet because I wanted to savor being pregnant a little while longer, since I knew my life would be forever changed...and I didn't yet know how, and I was a little nervous about the whole process...and then I realized that the baby is going to come out one way or another. And I wouldn't really be in charge anymore, and I wouldn't be for a long time, if ever, really.

So, all I will say on this subject is something my mom told me: "It's called labor for a reason." It's work. Sometimes it's very hard work. But it's women's work: we've been doing it since the beginning of time and we'll be doing it until the end of time. We were designed to do it. But that in no way diminishes the fact that every baby is no less than a tiny miracle.

Living large

I walked into the post office and the clerk greeted me cheerily and asked me when I was due.

What a wonderful question when you are actually pregnant.

What a horrible thing to hear when you are pushing your newborn in the stroller. So, I said, "I'm not, I already had the baby…" And I tactfully left off the rest of the sentence "…you @$*&ing dolt—can't you see him *right here in front of me* in the stroller?"

I had heard things like this a handful of times after Mark was born—"Are you pregnant again…already?" It got tiring trying to hold my stomach in all the time, and I was *really* tired after I had Baby Chase—so tired that I tended to slouch. I was actually concerned that something was *very* wrong with my stomach muscles because of the way they bulged even when I tried as hard as I could to hold them in. (Was there such a thing as irreversible separation? Maybe I needed a surgical correction?)

I had tried on post-partum support devices at the Motherhood Maternity store in the mall and couldn't get even the ultra-plus-grande size to come near to closing around my waist. If I could, I would not need the device, right? Isn't it kind of pointless to make girdles in small sizes? I can't stand looking at the models in catalogs wearing them—they are the last people who need them!

And I suppose I should reevaluate the benefits of wearing maternity shirts. They sure were comfortable, but if people were going to mistake me for being pregnant, then no thanks. However, if I wore my regular wardrobe, the girth of my belly would have been accentuated by the snugness of the garment. Would people then think I was pregnant or that I had a beer belly? Which would be worse? Hmmm...(I imagine pregnant *and* beer belly would be the worst.)

I digress. Back to the post office...I was going to just let the clerk's comment slide, but she continued (yes, *she*—I would have thought someone of the same gender, who, come to find out, *has* a child of her own—would be a little more empathetic): "Oh, you can't always tell...you look four months pregnant."

Hello!? Could you stick your foot any farther into your mouth?

"Do you have any love stamps?" I asked, in order to change the subject (and my attitude).

Young (at heart, anyway)

I was having a conversation with one of my childhood friends, and she brought up someone who didn't have children and said, "I guess she never wanted to grow up."

And I said, "Bummer for her, she doesn't know what she's missing." After a brief silence, I added, "But what do you mean 'grow up?' Having kids makes me feel younger."

"Oh not me," she said. "I had to grow up!"

And I asked, "What do you mean, you feel *old*?"

"Not just that, more like I had to get responsible."

"Oh," was all I could think of to say.

During the long pause that followed, I realized that I had already become responsible by the time I had kids (which is why my kids are six-plus years younger than her kids—it took me that much longer to get it together).

It's true that I've become somewhat more staid in that doing risky and adventurous things does not appeal to me anymore—like sledding, skiing, riding on motorcycles, or inline skating—these things are reserved for the invincible youth, a demographic with which I no longer identify. I have to face the fact that I am probably not ever going to see the world while working on a cruise ship, either.

And while I acquiesced that it was only since I had children that I *always* wore my seatbelt, usually drove the speed limit, and only crossed in crosswalks, I could much more easily entertain the "old versus young" aspect.

Especially right then—I felt tired, beat, like a bag of bones—creaky and...old. I could no longer pull all-nighters without suffering the consequences.

At the same time, often I feel *younger* because I get the privilege and joy of rediscovering the world: the way Mark's eyes light up at such simple pleasures as bubbles, the sound of airplanes or birds, favorite toys, a new toy or often things that were never meant to be toys but suddenly are...or even just the play of shadows against the wall (something that held Baby Chase's rapt attention)... I get to sing, skip, use crayons, watch Sesame Street and The Electric Company (a favorite from my own childhood, which I found on some obscure cable channel at 4:00 a.m.), and go to the playground and library. We have playdates! And naps—something that probably thrills me more than it does the boybies. These are treats that I can enjoy, too. It reminds me not to be so jaded, not to take things for granted. I get to be a kid again.

I asked my friend, "Is 'grown up kid' an oxymoron?"

Keeping it together

"Cut the bagel, cut the bagel, cut the bagel," I chanted to myself (not silently) as I got up from the computer. It was 10 a.m. and I hadn't eaten yet, except for coffee and juice, and I'd been up since 6:00 a.m. (relatively late these days).

Lately if I don't remind myself of things by making lists (verbal as well as the more familiar written), I might forget to do them at all. And then the boybies wake up from their naps and it's too late. Not much gets done when they're awake. I consider myself lucky if I can load the dishwasher, switch over the laundry, or go to the bathroom. If I'm really lucky, I can check my e-mail, but I have to think twice about answering the phone, and never the business line.

Chanting works, but only for short-term things. Cutting the bagel is only one step of the process—hopefully that first step will trigger the next logical steps, but that is not always so. Usually, if I cut it, it makes it into the toaster, but it might stay there forever (or at least several hours). I actually have to remind myself "knife and paper towel." The knife and paper towel (note this is not "plate." "Plate" does not wrap around bagel for easy consumption in front of one's computer or in the car) is the next step after toasting, and hopefully that will trigger the third step, which is getting out the cream cheese. Eating it is actually the final step.

I have actually walked upstairs repeating three things (e.g., wipes, plastic bag, outfit), reached the top of the stairs and become totally sidetracked, so that I end up back downstairs without those essential go-bag refill items. (Just keeping the diaper bag filled is a lesson in list management, and if it isn't fully stocked, going anyplace could become a major ordeal, if not a downright catastrophe.)

My written lists are pretty much ongoing. There are grocery and other to-buy lists on the counter that I add to until a trip to the store becomes imperative. Then I have the list in my day planner of things to do. In the past, I've had to rewrite half of them on the next day, and maybe on the next. But since I now have a two-pages-per-week style of planner (down from two pages per *day* when I was a "very busy" outside salesperson) I write the item anywhere on the two pages and hope I don't have to rewrite it for the following week.

Action items that don't have any specific deadline (when monkeys freeze over), I write on a sticky note and paste somewhere on my desk or computer. The problem with this is I have become just as immune to these as I have the banner ads and pop up windows all over my Internet browser.

Here's what the sticky notes on and around my desk said at the time of this writing:

Two of them stuck together side by side contain three different passwords for various Internet sites (written across both of them, so if I lost one, the remaining one would be rendered useless)

One is Baby Chase's social security number. I think this was supposed to remind me that I need to open a bank account for him—and I better hurry because he is already six weeks old. Time is money, after all!

Another has our pediatrician's insurance provider number. This is meant to prompt me to call the insurance company and let them know who is Baby Chase's official doctor.

Five of them contain a mixed assortment of things including story ideas, phone numbers, and a website I wanted to visit for some reason that I can't remember and the name isn't intuitive.

One says "hibernate" and I have to try to remember what that means.

Then there's "3:30 Get Mark." As if I would forget to pick up my son (though this has happened in some of my nightmares)!

And I can't forget the one stuck to my checkbook that is reminding me to verify that I can cover a check I wrote without transferring money. This probably falls into the category of "pressing."

Verbal and written lists are the most effective ways I know to keep it together. Many times I use the two in conjunction as I find myself chanting what I should write on a list.

Softheartening

I didn't want to wish time away, but I was just *not* having fun. It was mere weeks after Baby Chase was born and it had been so hot, it was hard to keep my cool—literally and figuratively. We did not have air conditioning. I had said numerous times that I couldn't wait for the summer to be over. I searched for something to be grateful for because "at least I'm not pregnant" wasn't doing the trick anymore.

Mark had a full day of daycare on Tuesdays and Thursdays—because I am flexible workwise, I agreed to give this a shot. It turned out to be just too much for him. He was only 18 months old. He would come home cranky and tired. And if Baby Chase cried, Mark would cry even louder because he knew I would have to pay attention to the baby. I really could have used more help during "witching hour," but it had been so hot in the house that I was reluctant to ask anyone to come over because it was so uncomfortable for them.

I had forgotten how awesome—and time consuming, and frustrating, and exhausting—it is to have a little being so completely dependent on me, whose life is literally in my hands. Baby Chase was hungry all the time, and nobody but Mommy can breastfeed. And I had forgotten how such a tiny bottom could wreak so much havoc. I suffered numerous double-diaper changes (finally getting a new diaper on and Baby poops again…I had to remember to wait for the "third wave"), or mid-change poops where either the changing table became a mess or Baby's socks landed in poop as if drawn by a magnetized force…or, if I got to the point where I was congratulating myself on catching the poop in the diaper, Baby would pee on himself, and/or the wall, and/or me. The sheer volume of laundry was astounding.

I would have thought that having been through it before I would be used to it, but it seemed like adding a new baby more than doubled the work. Sometimes I thought, "Oh, my gosh, what have I done!?"

People told me, "Don't wish the time away. Enjoy them while they're young." But I felt completely overwhelmed.

I kept telling myself that everything would be better when Baby Chase was three months old and had a more predictable schedule (which would include part-time daycare) or six months old and could sit up by himself and reach for and hold his own toys and baba. (That's still "young," right? Surely things would be more enjoyable then…)

Then I tried looking at it a different way. Every time I felt annoyed because I was nursing around the clock and irritable because I often had a screaming toddler vying for my attention simultaneously, I would endeavor to remind myself, "It won't be this way forever." Someday Baby Chase will sleep through the night in his own bed, just like Mark. Someday they will even play together. And then my mind would fast-forward through their school years—recess, field trips, show and tell, hot lunch, after-school sports, first dates, graduation; then into adulthood—going to college and/or getting a job, getting married, and having kids of their own. I'd be a grandmother! Someday they aren't going to want to hang out with Mommy at all anymore…not like they do today, anyway.

I clung to these thoughts whenever I felt beleaguered by boybies. (Frequently.)

My summer vacation

Daddy and I were looking over the hospital bill from my stay with Baby Chase. It was about 10 times higher than we expected—but it was correct. I had confirmed that much with the insurance company.

I *had* requested a private room, as I had done with Mark, but this time around I was in the hospital longer because I'd had a C-section, and we also had different insurance, and who knows … the hospital may have changed its rates.

Anyway, Daddy said, "Well, you could always count that as your vacation. Ha ha. Snort." (Daddy had just returned from *his* vacation with his three older children.)

I said, "Ha ha."

Then silence as we thought about his comment. Then we both spoke, simultaneously.

He said, "Bummer that didn't include airfare." And I said, "Well, I did get three squares a day."

A vacation in the hospital seemed absurd to me, but as I thought about it some more, considering what my last few vacations were really like (not to mention life at home), this one wasn't so bad!

My most recent "vacation" was a trip to California to visit family with my mom and Mark when I was 32 weeks pregnant with Baby Chase and Mark was almost 15 months old. We did get Mark has own seat on the airplane (I certainly didn't have a lap anymore!) but he was no picnic to manage. He just didn't want to sit in his seat and I can only imagine how boring it must have been for the little guy to stare straight ahead at the back of the seat in front of him for six hours. And most of our activities had to be scheduled around Mark's naps. Certain events like lunch in a restaurant wouldn't be enjoyable for anyone if he was overtired.

Before that, Daddy and I took Mark on a cruise to Bermuda. He was only four months old at that time. He was quite a hit on board the ship, but again, it was a lot of work to manage him. We wound up eating at the outdoor buffet for just about every meal, and couldn't enjoy the nightlife. We watched lots of movies in our postage-stamp-sized cabin with the volume really low.

Sometime between Bermuda and California, Daddy and I left Mark with Grandma and went to a remote all-inclusive resort in St. Kitt's during the week Daddy decided to start a new diet. He had a hard time coping with the fact that the resort didn't serve all the food on his new diet because that was also the week he decided to quit smoking. Again.

So, back to my hospital visit, aside from the fact that I had a new baby via major abdominal surgery, it fit all the criteria of a good vacation: room service, friendly and professional staff on call to attend to all manner of personal needs, and the whole thing was a blur (thanks to the drugs I took every four hours like clockwork). And like all good vacations, it was over way too soon.

All joking aside though, I wondered if this is a common cliché that mothers only get a break when they're in the hospital giving birth. And, like, welcome to the club?

The twilight zone of roles

I'm a work-at-home-mom. Of course, all moms are work-at-home moms—I know that now—but what I mean by that is that I do my job from home. Except it's not really a job the way most people know it. I'm a freelance technology writer.

I didn't take any time off from work after the boybies were born. When you're a freelancer, there is no paid maternity leave—if you don't work, you don't get paid. Many times I'd be typing with one hand while I had a baby lying across my lap. (After Baby Chase arrived, I had enough sense, however, to build longer review cycles into my project schedule).

When Mark was eight weeks old I began a major assignment: writing a series of articles for a corporate magazine. I wanted to do this particular project in order to feel like I was accomplishing something over which I had some modicum of control (unlike how I felt as a new mom). "I'll just work around Mark's nap schedule," I thought. "It's better for the baby to have a well-balanced mom." Truthfully, I wasn't ready to let go so abruptly of the business-minded person I was. And I *liked* working for money.

What was wrong with my reasoning was that I didn't have time to care for a new baby *and* work as much as I usually did. I wasn't at all balanced. As any new mother will tell you, there are just not enough hours in the day, even if I didn't sleep. Yet I couldn't imagine "just being a mom" because I didn't yet feel competent in my new role. And besides, homemakers are not even counted in the gross national product—I learned that in my college economics class.

Does that mean that what they do is not recognized as work? Hardly!

What I quickly found out was that being a mother is one tough job. You have a really demanding boss. There were many times that I was just exhausted, but I had to snap to attention regardless.

Rather than being well balanced, by adding a big freelance writing assignment into the equation, I tipped the scale in favor of temporary insanity. I might have been dividing my time equally, but it was among too many things! I could barely get an hour's time during the day to write anything coherent. And never mind the impromptu phone call for fact checking. Thank *God* for e-mail, where it's okay if you get interrupted. I wound up doing a lot of work at night. Fortunately, I did take someone's advice about not sending anything out for review until the next morning—what might have seemed clever at the time did not always make sense by daylight.

I made it through the project, but I will *never* try that again. I quickly realized that it's impossible to work at home without some sort of childcare, which I immediately arranged.

I refuse to participate in the debate about staying at home versus working, because I do both, and it's not so cut and dry. I share some of the same challenges as stay-at-home moms and some of the issues of mothers who work outside the home. I don't fit neatly into either niche.

Besides, as I mentioned, every mother is a working mother. What it really boils down to is working for a paycheck versus working without financial rewards…missing out on a lot of "firsts" that childcare providers are privileged to enjoy (whether they tell you or not) or losing contact with and the respect of former colleagues...and sometimes even relinquishing equal voting rights in their marriages (as a the by-product of less-than-equal financial contributions).

Recently, I was filling out a survey and had reached the end where you have to divulge all those demographic details. The survey asked, "Are you currently employed outside the home." The choices were "yes, full time," "yes, part time," "on maternity leave," and "no." None of the choices applied to me. I was stumped.

I would up checking "yes, part time" and handwriting a caveat that said "I work in my home office." I am sure there are other moms with such atypical solutions for blending work and family—it sure would be gratifying to be recognized. Even "other" or "none of the above" would be a start.

Style vs. comfort

One time I was wearing a pair of maternity pants (I had put the maternity shirts in the nether region of my closet not long after my chat with the post office clerk) and was on the fence about whether I should change before I went to pick up Mark. These pants were oh-so-very comfortable—yet *so* unflattering, and I didn't really have time to do the closet shuffle.

If I hiked them up as high as the fabric at the waist allowed (given my relatively small waistline in those days), then they sat right under my bust. If I let them sit below "the paunch," then the crotch hung down to my knees. If I rolled the waistband, it added a layer of padding around my middle (an area where I needed to be subtracting from, not adding to). Any of these options were just fine, but not for outdoor use.

Contemplating changing ended when I looked at the clock and saw that it was *time to go.* When I arrived at Mark's babysitter's, she was standing outside talking with a couple of her cul-de-sac neighbors, while all the kids scampered together on a colossal play structure. God, did I wish I had changed my pants then! When am I going to learn to pay attention to that still small voice?

Everyone else was wearing shorts sets and sandals (with painted toenails, of course) and looked cool and composed. The outfit I had on only served to illustrate that I don't get out much. Why was I even *wearing* pants when it was such a warm day? (Well, that's an easy one—because I probably hadn't shaved my legs in more than a week!)

"Note to self," I remember thinking. "*Never* wear these pants again!"

But the reason I was wearing them in the first place was because I didn't even own anything in the right size. I was reluctant to go out and buy new clothes in a bigger size because I was afraid that once I owned it, I would never get out of it.

When I finally broke down and acquired some new pants, come to find out, they weren't really even that comfortable. Nothing is as comfortable as maternity clothes. Except pajamas. And now that I am privy to this knowledge, I have I have begun wearing pajamas around the clock. I have casual pajamas for work or errands and dress pajamas for church or other important functions, and of course there are the pajamas I wear to bed (which I also may wear while exercising). All of the pajamas except the dress pajamas come in both short and long lengths. Form has officially taken a backseat to function.

My next wardrobe goal is to find some pajamas suitable for fall and winter. This could be a challenge since most pajamas feature some sort of delicate floral pattern reminiscent of the warmer seasons, however I may be able to reach my objective in a men's department.

I would just love to launch a clothing line for "maternity and beyond," because I am so sure that I am not the only one who doesn't wear her pre-pregnancy jeans home from the hospital.

Witching hour

I never knew there was such a thing as "witching hour" until I had a second baby and became outnumbered by my children. The true meaning of the term became apparent when both boybies needed me at the same time, usually at the end of the day. They sparred for my attention and their competition fed off itself. Every time Baby Chase cried, Mark would come running to me à la Teensy. But unlike Teensy, his concern was not to tell me Baby needed me, but to keep me from going to him at all.

Since Baby Chase was just an infant, I really couldn't ignore him. And Mark was a pre-conversational toddler, so I couldn't exactly explain to him that he had to wait. And anyway, waiting is almost as incomprehensible to an 18-month old as it is to an infant.

Baby Chase wanted to nurse constantly (and this was a defining factor that characterized witching hour), and would not tolerate a sling (this looks so good on other people, but just never worked for me) or any other carrier. Typically this period of non-stop nursing was between 5:00 and 7:00 p.m., the hours normally reserved for Mark's dinner, bath, and bed. (I can see why people wean subsequent babies early.) Therefore, I had one arm at best with which to manage Mark and everything else.

I had moved Mark out of his high chair and into a booster seat, but since I got him a mini table and chair set, he didn't want to sit at the kitchen table any more. The problem with the small table is that he got up at will, so often I would be chasing him around the house trying to get him to eat while holding Baby Chase. Not good. Mommy was no longer in charge when that happened. I have since relegated that table to our art projects.

And of course it was not really possible to nurse Baby Chase while bathing Mark. Often during bathtime, Baby Chase would serenade us with his nonstop crying from his nearby bouncy seat. He wanted to be held and cuddled. But even if I postponed Mark's routine, I couldn't sit and leisurely rock Baby Chase to sleep—Mark would be tearing through the house wreaking havoc. He had learned that I couldn't redirect him as easily if I was tending to Baby Chase.

I remember lamenting to my mom that it is so hard to be torn between two kids, one of whom was my one and only up until two months ago, who had no *idea* why Mommy was trying to "push him away." And the other was a helpless little baby that gazed at his big brother all starry-eyed (the same way he looked at everyone, really), who needed my protection.

"I know just how you feel," she replied. Of course she does. I have a younger brother (who is now known as "Uncle").

Many evenings all three of us ended up in tears. Often one of the boybies wore himself out crying, fell asleep, and our love triangle dissolved. Then the other two of us would collapse together, emotionally exhausted, spent—witching hour just a mere memory. Until the next day.

Breaking the rules

After Baby Chase was born, I kept him with me for most of our hospital stay. Invariably when a nurse came into the room, she'd find us in bed together cuddling. One of the nurses commented that he was a "snugglebug" when she walked in to find him sleeping face down on my chest yet again.

I remarked, "Yes, you're right. I don't know *how* I am ever going to get him to sleep on his back."

Silence. The nurse just looked at me. I felt like I had made the parenting gaffe du jour—all the nurses would be talking about it, I was sure.

Every one of the books I had read, the magazine articles, the newborn channel in the hospital, the video I took home, the pediatrician, the devices in the store to keep Baby in the "proper position" reinforce the idea that "Thou shalt put Baby to sleep on his back." The reminder was even printed on the front of size one Pampers diapers.

So one time, when I'd lamented to Daddy that I couldn't get Baby Chase to settle down for the night, he asked me if I had considered putting him to sleep on his stomach, I just said, "No."

Okay, I didn't *just* say "no."

I said, "NO!" Eyes opened wide, horrified.

Daddy simply said "Why not? He likes it."

I sputtered and grasped for a good answer. Daddy already had three kids; the youngest of whom was 10 when we had Mark. Just half a generation ago, things were done differently. I didn't really have a good reason 'why not' except for the fact that all the books I had read, the magazine articles, the newborn channel, the video I took home, the pediatrician, the device in the store to keep the baby in the "proper position" said so.

But the more I thought about it—and even though all the authorities suggest "back to sleep"—I realized that on-the-stomach is how everyone had done it up until not-so-long ago…so why was I being such a weenie?

Besides, Baby Chase was not in the category of babies susceptible to SIDS. And I was just so tired of carrying him around all the time, usually slung over my shoulder. He was a *big* boy.

Furthermore, I reasoned, since it definitely took more than twice as long to accomplish things with half as many hands—especially typing—I put him down for his naps on his tummy the next day.

It worked. He began sleeping for more than 20 minutes at a time. (Thank God!)

I justified that rather than doing everything "by the book," it was important for me to have a workable solution. I had exhausted myself with middle-of-the-night feedings with Mark, going through the whole ritual of feed, burp, change, repeat, repeat. With Baby Chase, frequently I just slept with him in the twin bed in his room (also not recommended by pediatricians or other moms who have said "watch out—he'll expect to sleep with you forever," but—au contraire—he sleeps just fine in his own bed now). He wore Huggies

Overnites from the beginning and I didn't change them during the night unless he had pooped.

As I look back, I can think of several things that I omitted confessing to our pediatrician. I didn't intentionally go against medical advice, nor would I ever advise doing so; I simply needed to learn to trust myself as a parent, and to learn from people who have been parents longer than me. I had to give myself permission to do what works for my family.

And I later realized that nurses have to be really careful about what they say, even if they speak from personal experience, because they must make sure they promote current AAP recommendations.

Drudgery

"I just don't know what's up with this baby," I sighed to my friend. "He doesn't want to eat, he's not tired, he doesn't have a bubble, and I just changed his pants."

"Maybe he wants to play," she said.

I gasped. And paused. "Oh," I sighed as I let out my breath. "Right."

I hadn't even considered that. I was burnt out. Baby Chase was almost three months old. Of course, he was getting to the age where he is going to do more than just eat, sleep, cry, and eliminate waste.

I realized that I had been all caught up in the drudgery part of parenting and I told myself I should slow down and enjoy my children. Then I felt bad about all the energy I had been putting into other things besides the boybies: my work, attempting to keep the house neat (despite recommendations to let that go, because frankly, my life feels even more complicated and chaotic when the house is a mess), and volunteer efforts for church. This stuff was taking me away from my kids.

While I do believe that babies and children should fit in to the structure of a family, I didn't realize at that time how much the existing structure of the family would be forced to change. Ours was still in flux, and as I have come to learn, change can be painful.

Get out much?

One day in the fall of 2001, I was outside putting something in my mailbox. The fact that I actually made it out there before the mailman came was a bright spot in my otherwise Eeyore day. I looked up and saw my neighbor across the street, but I didn't wave or anything, convincing myself that he was probably busy. In fact, I was relieved that he didn't see me as I had old gray sweats with paint stains on them and a baggy white shirt that stuck out from underneath my baggy pink and white striped sweater, and I'd slipped flip flops on over my baggy white socks (I'd wear flip flops year round if it wasn't such a fashion faux pas). I turned around quickly and headed back to the house.

As I was approaching the front porch, I noticed that the mums were dying—dead actually—and I felt about as droopy and dried up as they looked when I picked them up, planning to heave them in the compost pile in the back yard (with all the lawn trimmings that made up the majority of the compost, since I never quite could make it out there with the nutrient-rich kitchen garbage that really belonged there).

Just then, the neighbor called over and initiated conversation, stopping me in my tracks. I found this interesting, because he often leaves the social niceties up to his wife.

Rather than yell across the street, I somewhat sheepishly walked over clutching my pot of withered mums and said, "Nice day, isn't it?"

He said, "Yes! And it was *yesterday*, too." Big smile.

And I thought for a moment and said, "Oh, yeah, that's right," remembering that I'd had the windows open. "I haven't been getting out much." I added, lamely. (It just felt too hard to get the boybies changed and dressed and ready to go out. I hadn't had the resources to cajole, joke, reason, amuse, convince—and sometimes bribe—to get them into shirts, sweaters, pants, socks and shoes. Never mind the coats and hats.)

And my neighbor said he had noticed that (he was often outside tinkering in his yard or with his vehicles) and asked if everything was alright.

So touched was I by his fatherly concern that I would have likely burst into tears if I hadn't all of a sudden had the "a ha moment" about why I felt so blah. I hadn't been out walking with the babies since the terrorist attacks—I had been caught up in watching the news for the past week and a half. And I hadn't felt like writing because I didn't think anything I had to say was important compared to what was going on in New York City and Washington, DC. I couldn't even remember leaving the house to do anything other than the requisite trip to church or the supermarket in I-didn't-know-how-long.

I knew I had to snap out of the doldrums and recoup my joie de vivre just as much for me as for my children. I had become a human doing (as opposed to a human being): on autopilot …watching life go by on the TV screen, caught up in the bad news of 9-11 and it's aftermath.

I exchanged pleasantries with my neighbor and wished him a good day as I returned to my day, my step a little lighter and springier than it had been.

And I vowed to make a conscious attempt to be more fully

present in my own life and the lives of my children. I have not watched the news since. While that may sound like I don't have a very expansive world view, I have found that if there is something important happening, I'll hear about it.

Not babysitting

I was trying to leave the project kickoff meeting discreetly. It was scheduled to begin at 9:30, but didn't get started until after 10:00 because a couple of the writers were late (we all get signed in and escorted to the conference room as a group).

I had allocated time until 11:30. I figured two hours is long enough for *any* business meeting. At least that is how I justified it to myself when I was unable to get extra care for both boybies at daycare.

So I had told the meeting coordinator in advance that I could stay until 11:30 and that if we hadn't concluded by then, I would like to make sure I walked out with my assignments, and that I would like to handle my departure as unobtrusively as possible.

I kept an eye on the clock. It was approaching 11:30 and the meeting showed no signs of ending. As I was packing up, the woman next to me, who, incidentally, was one of the tardy ones, said, "Are you going home to babysit?"

I was flabbergasted and momentarily speechless. I wished I had one of those MAD Magazine *Snappy Answers to Stupid Questions* books for working mothers.

What I said was, "It's not called babysitting when they're your children."

What I *wanted* to say was…something that I can't put in print because I know I'll live to regret it, which is why I did not say it to begin with. (And of course, I was trying to leave without causing a scene.)

I left the conference room with a barely perceptible nod and smile to the meeting coordinator and the sign language to indicate that I'd be in touch about qualifying the last two articles that we hadn't discussed yet.

When I was signing out, the receptionist said, "Is your meeting done?" (We had had the chance to get chummy beforehand, since *I* was the first one to show up.)

I said, "Not yet, but I am," with a big smile.

Truthfully, I did not have to go get the boybies at daycare. Daddy had decided to work from home that day and had agreed to pick them up at lunchtime. I didn't know that when I told the meeting coordinator I had to leave at 11:30. But, I still believe that two hours is long enough for any business meeting, and it was as much time as I was willing to part with. So I stuck to my guns and left.

A fellow freelancing mom, when I related the story to her said, "Don't give it 17 seconds." (I think she must have read someone's time management and/or motivational theory recently because I recalled her saying this about something else that she deemed unworthy of worry.) I tried to put it out of my mind but obviously it is still disturbing me. It felt like a jab, an indirect way to insult me, an insinuation that I was less-than...professional. What a disappointingly condescending thing to hear coming from one of my "sisters." I guess it just goes to show that there is absolutely *no way* you can know what it is like to be a parent until you are one. And since this woman does not have kids, we are simply not on the same wavelength.

BrotherMorphosis

Mark and I were sitting in the rocking chair in his room, gearing up for nunnight. Bedtime couldn't happen soon enough as far as I was concerned. I think Mark even felt that way because he didn't play "the sheet game" (where I attempt to make the bed with him jumping up and down on it and being bound under the bottom sheet as I tuck it in and/or diving under the top sheet after I've tossed it into the air and it's parachuting down) with his usual gusto and even *asked* me to put him to bed. No story. Bath time had been an unpleasant affair, bereft of most of the usual rituals including shampooing and bubbles… toothbrush teed up but left unused on the side of the sink. We had almost made it through a really hard day of what seemed to be the never-ending tantrum.

The storm we just rode out was at least the sixth of the day—and he was at school all morning! Lasting anywhere from 15 to 30 minutes, these spells were not merely annoying, they were a monumental test of my sanity and well being.

Saying "no" to Mark would set him off, but what else could I say when he intentionally dropped things in the toilet, swept all my makeup and toiletries off the counter, and rummaged under Daddy's sink, which had not been child-proofed. I had to say it again later when he wanted to color on anything but the paper I put down on his table and when he opened the dishwasher and tried to get in it (and if I pushed it closed so it latched, he turned it on). And by the time we got to grabbing the floor lamps and shaking them, opening my desk drawers and pulling files out, as well as the old favorite, let's-make-paper-come-out-of-the-fax-machine game (which was sometimes funny but not that day), I'd about had it.

At one point, I wound up sitting on the floor crying after I had told Mark, "Put the raisins in the trash, please" (that he had tossed on the floor during breakfast). I bellowed at him after I had tried to ask nicely what seemed like 50 times, all the while being told "noNoNOOOOoooo!"

I tried with all my might to regroup while Mark threw himself on the floor face down and wept. I had been up countless times the previous night with Baby Chase and now he, too, was crying. All I was trying to do was instill the lesson "if raisins are on the floor because you put them there on purpose, you need to pick them up." (He cleans up at school; I have seen him do it.) I was not proud that I yelled. In fact, I felt horrible.

Even when I was able to regain my composure, which used up what seemed like the rest of my reserves, I'm certain I was not able to keep from sighing or eyeball-rolling, which made me feel guilty on top of incapable.

Just when I had figured out the whole feeding, sleeping, bathing routine, I had to become a child psychologist. Nothing I had read prepared me for something like this. Never mind those "What to Expect" books. I needed to read something about discipline! Even talking to my friends hadn't really helped. Either they were not experiencing the same thing and never have, or they were lying.

It didn't help me feel any better about the situation when his teacher said "Mark had a wonderful day today." Why was it that he completely melted down when he got home?

I wondered if I was being too strict. Or maybe I was being too lax. Maybe he needed clearer guidelines. Did he not understand what I was asking of him? Was I asking too much? We were finally at the point where we are able to communicate about simple things. So was he mad that I understood what he wanted and said no anyway? It sure would be a lot easier to continue to clean up his messes and let him remain the untamed bundle of exuberance that a baby is, but what kind of parent would I be if I didn't socialize the boy. That's part of a parent's job, right?

I could pinpoint the exact day that the difficulties began in earnest. It was the day I had taken Baby Chase to do our Mommy-Baby portrait (which of course, I had also done with Mark when he was a baby), about a week prior. When I picked Mark up from his babysitter's house, she described behavior that I would call sulking—not eating, not smiling, refusing to make eye contact. Feeling guilty, I thought immediately, "Oh, no—he heard me tell Baby Chase that we were going to do something special together that day." (Usually when I am getting the boybies ready for the day I tell them what they can expect.). Then I thought again, "No, impossible...he must have a little cold that is making him irritable."

Well, he *did* have a little cold, but he was so uncharacteristically irritable that by the time Friday rolled around I was at the doctor's office with him. Doc said he had a slight ear infection, not even worth treating. This is the new custom today—let it go away by itself. However, in the four days since we had our visit, we had some all-out tantrums. The one that included head banging (against the side of the crib) even freaked out Daddy, the veteran father, who, thinking Mark was having a seizure, carried him downstairs and deposited him in my lap.

That made me worried because usually nothing fazes Daddy, not even the middle-of-the-night croup where I was ready to call the hospital. So we ended up back at the doctor's office. I figured, "Okay, his ear infection *must* have blossomed." But nope, nothing was physically wrong.

Where did these tyrannical spells come from? How does an ordinarily sweet-tempered, good-humored little boy transform into an unrecognizable I-gave-birth-to-that? monster?

I tried to get inside the mind of my son as we sat there and rocked. I told myself, he feels secure with me—that's why he can flatter me with his worst behavior. He's especially independent, this is why he gets *especially* frustrated when I thwart is desires. After all, he doesn't understand why it is not appropriate to eat dessert for breakfast, throw his food on the floor, yank at his baby brother to get out of "his" bouncy seat, or step out into the street without holding my hand.

I thought back to one night not long after Baby Chase's arrival, Mark was playing with his Amy and I began asking him questions like, "Marky, where's the baby's nose, mouth, hair, foot, knee…?" and he kept pointing to himself. He clearly still considered himself "The Baby."

Of course no matter how big he gets, he will always be my baby. But next to Baby Chase, he had suddenly—and against his will—become a little boy. He must have felt displaced, and literally, he was. He was usually the one who got handed off. How much of his behavior was related to the fact that he was a toddler and how much was simply his BrotherMorphosis?

I was holding Mark in my arms and even though I had wanted nothing more than to put him in his crib, shut the door, and have some peace and quiet when he finally fell asleep, once he did, I was paralyzed.

I just sat there rocking with him, listening to his little breaths, and admiring the way his lush eyelashes brushed his cheeks where not long before angry tears had overflown.

My beauty regimen, then and now

Gone are the days of makeup, hot rollers, and painted nails.

I used to wonder what one item of makeup I just couldn't do without, if I were forced to choose just one (this must have been a survey I saw in a magazine once because I sure wouldn't have dreamed it up on my own, nor do I have the time to bother pondering such inane ideas today). They were all essential, weren't they?

Don't get me wrong, I was no painted lady, but I just didn't feel complete without makeup—natural looking of course—just enough so I looked polished and put together. I did my nails myself once a week or so. And I would put hot rollers in my hair almost every morning while I applied my makeup and/or touched up my manicure.

Now, after children, I typically wash my face with a baby wipe, use Visine, and apply lip balm—if I can find it and if Mark hasn't dug the contents out (with his little fingers that fit perfectly into a tube of lip product) and smeared them somewhere.

My real makeup has become reduced to something I offer as an amusement or diversion to Mark while I am trying to get something done, like take a shower or pack our go-bag.

My nails are now bare and cut very short so as not to inadvertently scratch anyone or accumulate too much diaper cream beneath them. And since I wind up washing my hands so often, my nails are somewhat fragile. And in the winter, I actually have to wear lotion and cotton gloves to bed or my hands get so chapped they have been known to crack and bleed, which is even less attractive than the Disney-character look (I assure Daddy every time he comments).

For my hair-do, I employ a scrunchie or clip. After Mark was born, I tried having my hair cut shorter, in an actual "style," so that I could wear it down, but I just wound up using more clips to put it up. (I can't have hair available for little hands to grab.) Sometimes I mix things up with barrettes or bubble elastics, but it is not long before I return to the old standbys.

I think I now understand why "grown-up hair" is short hair. Someone told me once that every woman over 30 is supposed to have short hair (not touching her shoulders). I wonder if that is a real rule, or just something that evolved out of convenience (in the days before scrunchies and clips) because most mothers were mothers by the time they were 30?

After having my hair highlighted for several years, I resumed being a brunette and was subsequently told by a handful of people how *nice* my hair looked when it was highlighted. (Gee, thanks.) Reverting to my natural color was just…natural…because a) it is supposedly not safe to color your hair when pregnant and b) it is not easy to find the time to do it after a baby is born and c) not even possible to find the time after the second comes along.

Another naturally occurring phenomenon was the emerging patch of weird-textured gray hair at the front-and-center of my head—right where my bangs began. This patch started as a few little spikes, which I used to pluck.

My hairdresser admonished me, "Don't pluck a gray, two

will grow back in its place." (This sounded hinky to me so after noodling it for a while, I realized it couldn't possibly be true or people who were balding would pluck in order to reverse their hair loss.) The only reason I quit plucking is that you can only pluck so many before a patch of scalp would replace the patch of gray ... so I chose gray over scalp.

Then I decided to cut my own bangs. I cut them a little farther back with the hopes that the gray would be lost in the middle of them. I figured that this would also camouflage the flyaway wisps that had recently sprouted at my temples. But somehow they fell in a clump like a horse's forelock, which required my having to use little clips and styling products to coax this hair back where it should have been if I hadn't cut off a foot of it.

When I wound up wearing ponytails just about every day and feeling really dowdy, I decided it was time to see my hairdresser again. I stopped in to make an appointment. I 'fessed up about cutting my own bangs. "Of course you did..." she said kindheartedly (since I hadn't been there in so long), and my sin was forgiven. I just knew that all my beauty problems would be solved.

They weren't, but it's amazing how uplifting a trip to the salon can be.

Weaning

It was 5:15 in the morning and I was downstairs fixing a bottle for Baby Chase.

I felt very sad about this.

Baby Chase was only four-and-a-half months old. I had thought that I could nurse him a lot longer than that, longer even than Mark. (We had made it all the way to six-and-a-half months). Maybe I could even make it to one year or beyond, as recommended by pediatricians everywhere. I was really committed. Especially because I thought it was probably the last time I would ever nurse a baby.

Breastfeeding had been going great since day one. Baby Chase ate well and frequently. He was gaining weight at a phenomenal rate. At his two-month visit, he weighed a remarkable 16 lbs. 5 oz.

When he began daycare, I pumped breast milk for the first few weeks. But pumping became increasingly difficult, because as it worked out, the most efficient time to do it was when Baby Chase was nursing. It wasn't easy to nurse, pump, and fend off Mark simultaneously.

I read somewhere that as soon as you introduce the bottle, the weaning process has begun. I could see how that might be the case. Once it became an option, sometimes I offered a bottle instead of nursing. It was just practical when I was trying to juggle both boybies, especially during witching hour.

And then, I had to manage my obsession about waste and/or improper handling. Even though the teachers at our daycare were extremely well educated and conscientious, I don't think anyone respects breast milk as much as the mom (and the baby, of course). It's nothing to toss out a couple of ounces of formula at the end of a bottle, but with breast milk … I cringe at the thought! It was truly the beginning of the end when I figured it would be just as easy to give Baby Chase formula at daycare—one or two feedings a day—and nurse the rest of the time.

So, then I was down to nursing maybe four or so times a day: once in the morning when we got up, once in the early afternoon, and twice at night, sometimes three times.

But, pretty soon, as Baby Chase became more and more aware, nursing in the daytime became more and more impossible. He'd want to look around the room. The trouble with that was, he also wanted to stay latched on. It was painful for me and frustrating for him. He would tug and kick and flail his little arms. It's not like I could pick up and go to a quiet room whenever I wanted, as is suggested. I couldn't just leave Mark alone. Not only would he howl at the insult, but also, it was dangerous because who knew what kind of mischief he'd get into.

"Okay," I rationalized, "I'll just nurse at night, and in the afternoon if he's hungry when Mark is napping." (That way Mark wouldn't know I was cheating on him.) But this was a mixed blessing because I had been trying to get the boybies on the same schedule so I could have some time to do things—like work—in the afternoon.

We went on like this for a while …and I became absolutely exhausted, waiting until 11:00 to go to bed so I could nurse and then getting up one or two other times (I was never really sure because I was sleepwalking). I told myself it was worth it because I didn't want to give up breastfeeding.

Until the fateful night.

Perhaps it was the beginning of a growth spurt. Baby Chase had gone to bed at 5:00 p.m. and usually he'd sleep until at least 10, often 11. Well, he woke up at 7:15, before I had even put Mark to bed. So of course I gave him a bottle and figured he'd go a lot later than 10 or 11 and that I should just go to sleep that night rather than wait for him to wake up for his late-evening feeding.

No such luck. He woke up at 10:45. We nursed. Then he woke up again at 1:00 a.m. We tried nursing again. He cried in frustration: supply just *wasn't* meeting demand. I tried rocking him, I tried walking around with him, then I tried nursing again. It was 1:30 by that point. No luck. I gave up and made a bottle. He drank it all down without stopping. I put him back to bed and he slept until 5:00 a.m., which brings us full circle. I *still* didn't have any milk for him. I went downstairs to make the bottle.

So much for my lofty one-year goal. I consoled myself with the thought that at least Baby Chase, at close to 20 pounds, was the *size* of some one-year olds. But it really wasn't only about him. I wasn't ready to face the fact that the nursing a baby part of my life was over and that is why when it came time to purge the nursing tops from my closet and bureau, they sat in the upstairs hallway for weeks. Before they went back up into the attic.

Moonlighting

"I've got some stuff to do before tomorrow morning," I said as I shrugged my coat on. My friend looked at me blankly for a moment, looked at her watch, and looked at me again with one eyebrow raised.

"What?" I said. "I've got a concall to prepare for and I told an editor I'd get him some samples."

It was a Thursday night. I was leaving my women's investment club annual holiday party. It was only half an hour before the "official" end time, but I knew it was going to go later than that because some of the women's husbands were on their way to "crash."

"You can't do it in the morning?"

"I don't have the luxury of procrastination any more. I've got two *little* kids."

"Oh-Kaaaayeeeeeee….." she said, dragging out the word and leaving the statement hanging for me to infer what she meant, which was certainly "your loss."

But not really. This is the winning-est scenario there is. This thought was reinforced as I called to mind the last time I tried getting up early to get something done.

On that particular day, I got up at 4:00 a.m. I know that sounds undesirable, and it was. It was still dark, but I was up, so I decided to get a head start on the day. After I nursed Baby Chase and put him back to bed, I made coffee, wrote out some cards, took a shower, and begin editing a document that I wanted to deliver that day.

I got the bags ready for daycare and loaded up the car while Mark ate breakfast. We sat together for a bit, him eating raisins (probably far too many) and me continuing to edit the aforementioned document. Then he announced "ah dah, ah dah, ah dah!" which meant "all done." He wanted to leave the table, until he saw that I had a pen in my hand. I tried to hand him some crayons, and the Grandparents' Day cards I had been trying to get him to "sign" for the past two days, but he insisted that he use the pen. So I finished editing in crayon. Mark proceeded to write all over his shirt, himself and the table and was insulted when I tried to get the cards beneath the pen.

Okay, enough. "Marky, want to watch Elmo while I go get Baby Chase ready?" (Baby was starting to stir—I could hear him on the monitor.)

While I was changing and dressing Baby Chase, I thought, "Hmmmm.... I wonder when he last pooped?" At one point in Baby Chase's short life I imagined that he must not have any intestines, because there was such a close correlation to his eating and eliminating. Every time I fed him I had to change his pants and it seemed like there was *always* a poop in there. He was like one of those drink and wet dolls with a direct route between his mouth and his bottom. But now he doesn't go every time he eats any more... in fact, he didn't go for a whole week before his baptism and I remember praying, "God, please let him poop *before* we don the heirloom white baptismal gown..." At any rate, I was wondering whether or not I needed to warn his teachers.

We joined Mark in the family room for the last half of Sesame Street. Baby Chase nursed contentedly for a while and when he stopped abruptly, I looked down. He had that sly look that babies make, where they tuck their chins, hunch their shoulders, furrow their brows a bit and glance side to side coyly, mouth in a little "O" with the edges ever-so-slightly turned up. He let out the first wave of poop.

I said, "Oh, Baby went poopoo" to Mark. We're starting to think about potty training (oops, I forgot, it's now called "potty *teaching*"). Baby Chase started cooing.

"Yes, Baby, very nice! You made poopoo!"

As wave number two arrived, I said, "Okay, Baby, let's go change your pants. Excuse us Marky, we're going to go get Baby some fresh pants and then we'll go to school!"

I carried Baby Chase upstairs in such a manner that I was not touching or pressing his diaper area in any way. (I would hate for that poop to squeeze out around his legs onto his fresh clothes.) I carefully laid him on the changing table to scope out the situation. I peeled the diaper back—"Ooooooooh! Wow Baby, you made *poo* poo!"—and put it back down as I reached for the wipes.

I knew it was going to be a messy job so I pulled out four wipes. I lifted Baby Chase's legs...then I lifted them higher...and then higher still, until he was practically hanging upside-down from my left hand as I peered under him. I saw that poop had indeed oozed out of his diaper and all the way up to the back of his Onesie...should I cut it off of him or can I roll it up in a way that I don't smear his back, shoulders, and head with poop while I am taking it off (this was before I knew that Onesies could be removed from the top down)? As I pondered the thought, Baby Chase extruded his third—and final—wave of poop. I caught it with the receiving blanket that was lining the changing table.

Then I got to work. The receiving blanket went right in the Diaper Genie—the stain would *never* have come out (and chances are, this particular blankie would probably have wound up next in the queue when I was packing the go-bag for church or a visit to the grandparents'). The Onesie was actually salvageable, though—it's that uncertain-of-the-sex-alternative-to-yellow green color—this particular-poop stain would hardly be noticeable. I tossed it in the bathroom sink and sprayed some Shout on it.

Meanwhile, Mark was getting impatient—it was time to go to "scoo scoo scoo!" he let me know in no uncertain terms, hollering to me from the family room.

I said, "Okay, okay let's go" (as I thought, "I'm *so* glad it's a school day") as I descended the stairs with Baby Chase.

But wait, did I smell poop?

Baby Chase watched, amused, as I began my battle with a toddler who seemingly had separation anxiety about parting with his poopy diaper.

Then, at last, we were ready to go, half an hour later than I had hoped. I was exasperated but trying to be cheerful, reiterating (singing even) to myself, "I'm just so glad it's a school day."

"Baby first, then Mark." I picked up Baby Chase and carried him down to the car and tucked him under a blankie. I went back for Mark and helped him into his jacket. At last, we were out the door, only to be stuck behind a school bus the whole way.

We arrived at daycare. Everyone in the toddler room was already engaged in an activity. Since Mark is usually the first or second one there, he was a little put off and needed to cling. We said goodbye after what seemed like 20 minutes, and then I handed Baby Chase off to the lead teacher in the infant room who asked me, "Could he be hungry?" I looked at him and noticed that he was gnawing on his hand.

"I suppose he could be," (after the poop he made this morning, he's probably got a hollow leg, I thought to myself—no need to warn her…he probably won't poop for days!) "but he'll have to have a bottle because I *really* have to go."

At last, I was free… but my spirits sank when I remembered I had some errands to do. I needed diapers and formula, I had to go to the post office, and I couldn't really put off grocery shopping any longer because the cats had been shadowing me all weekend to remind me that they didn't have their preferred brand of food. And since this meant that even when the boybies were at daycare or napping, I still wouldn't get a moment to myself, I chose to add shopping to the to-do list.

I returned home with bags and bags of groceries. I forgot what a mess the place was. Cheerios were all over the living room floor along with various other kid-related items, and breakfast remnants littered the table. The kitchen sink was full of little dishes and bottles and cups and binkies. I had to put the groceries away and deal with the mess in the bathroom sink as well as the usual mountain of laundry that confronted me. I couldn't ignore it as I walked by so I started a load before I hauled all of the groceries up the stairs. Multiple trips: my favorite checkout lady got in the habit of not filling the bags too full when I was pregnant—she didn't want me to strain myself. More bags equals more trips up and down the stairs, but I shouldn't complain, exercise is good for me, right?

As I was rushing through putting away the groceries and emptying the dishwasher (only to begin refilling it with the contents of the kitchen sink), I realized I had forgotten to use soap in that load of laundry. At least I thought I forgot. I wasn't 100% sure either way. So what that boiled down to was that I was back to square one on the laundry.

By the time I had cleared the decks, I had only one hour to finish editing the document, before I had to leave to pick up the boybies. I thought to myself, "No wonder I wind up working most nights!"

I just smiled at my friend and said, "Enjoy the rest of the party!"

The Mommy-brain myth

You know how people—sometimes even mothers themselves—make fun of mothers for being forgetful or absent-minded? Well, that is really disturbing to me.

Just think about all the extra things a mother has to remember and think about, never mind do!

For instance, keeping the go-bag filled with diapers, wipes, and other basic necessities. Performing calculations regarding the likelihood of use versus the extra bulk of these provisions as they relate to the occasions for which they are to be used. Keeping track of the occasions themselves. Packing lunches for school. Unpacking the lunch bags when they come home. Wiping them out if necessary. Cleaning the high chair (even under the seat pad) and the floor up to five times a day (and occasionally the wall, sliding glass door, and radiators). Wiping down the stroller. Cleaning out the bathtub. Hanging up the towels. Cleaning out the potty. Changing diapers and giving Baby an impromptu bath due to once oozed and now crusted "poop? I didn't smell any poop!" (Apparently Mommy has the only working nose in the house.) Brushing teeth (ideally) twice a day. Washing little hands before meals. And after meals. Acquiring, sorting, organizing, and washing little clothes. Thinking up activities so that no one watches too much TV all at once. Orchestrating and executing said activities. Cleaning up the aftermath. Spontaneous adaptation to the best-laid plans when the voicemail on the answering machine says, "a responsible adult needs to be home to accept delivery from Sears between 8:00 and 5:00 tomorrow." Making Daddy's birthday, Christmas, and Father's Day gifts and cards from the kids. Ditto any and all of Daddy's relatives' gifts and cards. And mailing them. Answering the calls: "Did you bring the camera?" "Mommmeeeee!!" "I need a sympathy card for ….." "Baby, NO!!" "Oh, do you have their address?" "Baby touch me!" "Do you have any stamps?" "Mamamamamamama!" "Didn't you reset the clocks?" "Babababa" "Where are all the C batteries?" "Whussahhhhhh? WhussAH!?" "Are we doing anything next Thursday night?" (Crash!) "Meow…" "Baby do dat, Mommy!" "Mamamamama Hah hahhhhhh hee! Diddeeee. DIDDEEE!" "Honey, did you know there's water on the floor." "Water, Mommy! Waterwaterwaterwaterwater! Baby do it!" "Baby!" "Maaaaaah!" "BA-BY!" "MAAAAAH!!" "AYI-AYIAYIAYIEEEEE!" As well as anything that might just "come up."

Add to all this any revenue-generating work in various stages of completion as well as the rest of the housework and wifework and the bottom line is, there are just too many things to think about.

Because of this is born the phenomenon that I call "task fragmentation"—getting several things started and in various stages of completion and seemingly walking around my house in circles (and it literally is in circles: a small circle around the butcher block island in the kitchen and a larger circle around the whole downstairs, because the rooms all connect) while I try to tick something off the to-do list.

"There is nothing more important than what I am doing right now," I will try to convince myself (as I bend over to do something *really* important like clean the catboxes). Yet, I usually feel like I'm in a hurry and I have trouble keeping my mind still. I could be doing one thing and thinking about the next five or more things on my list.

It is just lovely when it all comes together at the end of the day, but often times, I've noticed that the sun has gone down and I've still got a bunch of stuff half-done, thus perpetuating the Mommy-brain myth.

What's disturbing to me is that mommy-brain really has nothing to do with being forgetful or absent-minded, It's simply a matter of having so much to remember and think about and do!

She's come undone

"Did you know that you only have one earring on?" Mark's teacher asked me.

Thank God that's all it was—I was getting a little paranoid with her double-taking (did I have a Cheerio stuck in my hair, a boogie in my nose, or some sort of funky hoo hoo in my teeth?).

I replied, "Yes, actually, I did know that. I had left the pair on the bathroom counter and somehow—probably with the help of Teensy, our cat—one of them ended up downstairs on my desk. I had put the other one away long ago, and have been meaning to put this one away, but kept forgetting to bring it upstairs, so I figured I'd just wear it until it ended up in my jewelry box." (To make a short story long.)

I probably could have ended it after the "Yes." And judging by her "Uh-huh" expression, I felt foolish that I hadn't.

This just got me thinking about the number of things that are only half done in my house these days. On a good day, they all end up getting all the way done by the end of the day. But lately, I've felt like things are in a perpetual state of disarray.

Everywhere I look something is out of place. The dining room table is covered with the overflow from the butcher block island in the kitchen, which is strewn with two flower arrangements (one silk), assorted seasonal decorations: pumpkins, candles, a Halloween bucket with leftover candy, mail sorted into several piles, tissues, baby monitor, baby formula, toddler snacks, and probably crumbs.

And speaking of crumbs, I've been trying not to look at the kitchen floor all day. It's white, so everything shows! I never even drew the blinds in the family room today—it's easier not to confront the dust, plus no one will be spending any time in there in the daylight anyway. Random toys are all over the place. Things that Mark has thrown down the stairs remain on top of the little rug by the front door that is askew from the cat skidding on it as he takes flight from curious little hands (or the flying objects).

And then…there's the laundry. Generally I have five or six really big loads a week, which I process on Mondays, no doubt overstuffing the machine. I usually set the dial on "extra high" (I don't even know why there's such a setting as "low"—what would that be, like one outfit?). Sometimes I have barely recovered from the laundry of the week prior, and I find myself ready to begin all over again, starting with emptying the baskets of the last week's clean clothes and putting them away in drawers and not just stacked on the bureaus lest the carefully sorted little piles (of receiving blankets, bibs, and cloth diapers that I use for almost everything besides their originally intended purpose, t-shirts, pants, stuff that should get hung in the closets, one pile each of socks and Onesies, and random assorted things that might have been washed such as the cover to the bouncy seat, a teething toy, mittens or a hat) become one again. Once in a while I have to empty the dryer of the last load of "last week's" clothes—thank God I finally figured out what the "Touch Up" setting on the dryer is for—shaking the wrinkles out of clothes that have been sitting in there so long that I don't know if they're just cold or still wet.

And the ultimate worst thing is that my office tends to be the catchall room for things I don't otherwise know what to do with. I sit at my desk facing my computer, where everything is sorted and filed appropriately (except for my e-mail in box, where nothing gets filed and it's basically the electronic equivalent to one of the piles of paper on the floor in the corners) and try not to turn around or even use my peripheral vision or else I'd get distracted by the things half-done or undone.

The advice from parenting magazines: "Just let it go" really used to bug me. Because, I felt like if I just let it go, then the next thing would get let go and then the next thing and the next thing and so on and so on, and then it would become harder and harder to get anything done because I wouldn't know where to begin. I'd become paralyzed, and then I'd come undone.

Now that I've come to accept that the normal state of affairs is "undone," it doesn't bug me as much.

Enrichment

Nothing makes me happier—and sometimes more miserable—and sometimes both within the same breath—than my kids. I have never known joy so great, or love so deep as well as other things on the less positive end of the spectrum, like deflating frustration and sheer exhaustion. There are no greater gifts I have received in my life than my sons. Consider this conversation.

"Mommy," said Mark.

"Yes, honey?" I replied.

"Mommy."

"Yes, love."

"Mommy."

"Yes, my lovey."

"Mommy!"

"Yes, honey!?"

"MomME."

"Ye-e-e-es….."

"Mommy."

"Yes, honey!"

"Mo-o-o-o-o-o-o-o-ommy."

"YES, honey."

"MOMMY."

"YES, love!"

"Mommy!"

"Yes! Marky!"

"MOMMY!"

"Marky!"

"Mo-o-o-o-o-o-ommy."

"Ma-a-a-a-a-rk."

"Mommy!"

"Mark!"

"Mommy!Mommy!Mommy!"

"Mark!Mark!Mark!"

"Mommy!"

"Yes, love, what is it!?"

"Mommy."

"Ye-e-e-es…..hone-e-e-e-e-ey…………..?"

"Mommy."

"What, honey?"

"Mommy?"

"What, honey."

"Mommy!"

"What, honey!"

"Mommy. Mommy. Mommy. MOM-ME!"

"WHAT, honey?"

"Mommy. Mommy. Mommy. MOM-ME!"

"WHAT! Mark!"

"MOMMY!"

(!!!!!@#$^%&) "WHAT!?"

"MOMMY!"

"WHAT! *Honey*. Tell Mommy! Please!"

"Mommy. Mommy Mo-o-o-o-mmmmmm-meeeeeeeeeeeeeeeeeee…………..."

WHAT! MARK! PLEASE! JUST! TELL! MOMMY!

MOMMY!

(gritting teeth, glaring) "WHAT!?"

"Mommy!"

(1,2,3,4…)

"Mo-o-o-o-o-o-o-o-o-mmeeeeee……

(5,6,7,8…)

"Mommy?"

(9,10. Deep breath. Smiling.) "Yes, honey, my love, my angel. What is it?"

"I wuv you, Mommy."

Holiday hangover

It was the Monday after Thanksgiving weekend. We had hosted 19 people at our house and I was still reeling in the aftermath. The alternative would have been to go somewhere not child-friendly (like where you can feel the host's eyes boring through you as you try to guide and direct the kids away from low-lying collectibles, the new rug, or the freshly painted walls and you're chasing them around the house saying, "no…no…*no*…NO!") which for a holiday like this, would be anywhere other than your own home. I never even considered a restaurant.

Because both boybies need their regularly scheduled naps, and since Thanksgiving is typically an extravaganza of lengthy duration, involving relatives who travel and expect to visit before, during, and after multiple sessions of eating, it was decided that we might as well host the event.

Daddy went hunting, which is a brand-new tradition, and left me to get the turkey in the oven (and I lamented that I had not made the stuffing the night before) as well as all the other various and sundry things one does to prepare a meal for 19 people. I remember trying to figure this out the year prior when we only had 14 people and praying I could get things underway before Mark woke up from his morning nap. But this year, I had *two* babies' schedules with which to concern myself. Fortunately, I had the good sense to ask my mother to come over early to help me.

The boybies had been either wrapped around my legs or tugging on my clothes or holding their arms out to me all day as I tried to prepare and pass food. It was next to impossible to have any semblance of meaningful conversation with grownups.

I suppose that they were just as stressed out as I was. Imagine if numerous people that you didn't know yet (or remember) who were six times (or more) your size wanted to look at you, talk to (and at) you, hold you, squeeze you, play with you, feed you, orchestrate the perfect photo of you...just imagine how exhausting that would be! I am surprised that five-month-old Baby Chase didn't come down with some bizarre illness between drinking his first soda, eating things (other firsts, no doubt) that may have been handed to him or that he had found on the floor, and someone working her finger around in his mouth asking him if he was teething. (He would probably have been too surprised to answer even if he could have...plus his mouth was full.)

We had a buffet-style dinner because while our dining room table is big, it sure isn't big enough for 19 people. It was a tight squeeze for the formal dinner for 14 the year before.

It took me three attempts to eat a plate of food between trying to play hostess, put Baby Chase to nunnight, and give Mark an impromptu bath, necessitated by the case of diarrhea he had seemed to acquire during the day. It was the type of holiday where I would have needed to watch the video of to actually experience, let alone appreciate, if anyone had made one.

So, there it was, Monday (again...sigh). I hadn't done any Christmas shopping yet, other than bookmarking a few websites and saving some things in online wishlists. I felt hungover and the holiday season was only just beginning.

The week from hell

"It just *can't* get any worse," I groaned to myself one Friday afternoon as I was *finally* getting Baby Chase down for his nap. Immediately I wanted to take it back because I was sure I had just jinxed myself. It turns out I did.

Daddy was 2000 or so miles away visiting his best friend. Baby Chase had been sick on and off for the previous couple of weeks, and very sick since midweek the week before when I finally took him to the doctor because he was "being a nudge." This is the only way I could describe it, because our usually cheery, happy-go-lucky baby just wasn't himself. It turned out he had not just one, but two, ear infections. I felt sorry that I hadn't called the doctor sooner, but he had just been in for his six-month visit a few days prior where he still had the same cold, with all the same symptoms, and no sign of *any* ear infections.

I had been on the fence about sending Baby Chase to daycare that morning, but I had a conference call scheduled. And since ear infections aren't catchy, and since he probably got the cold from one of the other kids there, anyway...off he went.

When I picked him up at noontime, he had a fever and diarrhea. One of his teachers had been trying to call me, but I was on my conference call agreeing to a heroically impossible (though I didn't know it at the time) deadline for a first draft of a technical white paper, so of course I did not answer. When I got there I felt just terrible.

I called the doctor's office for the third time in two days and was reminded that a fever is not always bad, which I knew, but I did not understand why he still had one when I had given him Motrin. (In retrospect, I probably underdosed him, considering his robust size). Our nurse, thought he could possibly have a virus in addition to his cold and ear infections.

And on top of it all, he had a diaper rash caused by the diarrhea he had spontaneously developed. I didn't know if the diarrhea was from the suspected virus, or if the antibiotics he was taking for the ear infections could have caused it. It was his first time taking any medicine like this, and he *did not* like it (though maybe that gagging thing that had started happening was *also* from the suspected virus).

Who really knew, and did the "why" matter when I was faced with so much "what?" I spent most of the weekend trying to keep poop and throw up—yes, the gagging had by then evolved to hurl—off of Baby Chase, the rugs, and me. And shoveling the driveway, but I don't want to get ahead of myself. Oh, and getting my period, which was most unwelcome after having gone just about two years straight without having it at all.

I was hoping Grandma would be able to take Mark to church Sunday morning, but when we got up, we were having "weather."

Mark said, "Rain!"

And I answered, "Well, yes, it's like rain, but it's colder. It's snow."

As it turned out, he was closer to the truth than I was. When it was time for Baby Chase to take his morning nap, Mark and I went "ow-SIGH!!" with the monitor and I shoveled while he traipsed around in the slush. It was very wet, heavy snow, and I felt idiotic shoveling it (none of the neighbors were—yet, anyway), because it seemed like it might melt and wash away, but I didn't want to take the chance that it would get colder before it was all gone, and that there would be a sheet of ice underneath the snow that was forecast for the next morning. I wanted to be *sure* I could get up out of the driveway (which is a little more than slightly inclined) to get the boybies to daycare on Monday.

I did not have any decent boots that fit. The ones I put on were suede and apparently whatever water repellant that had ever been sprayed on them had long since worn off. Or maybe my feet were just getting wet from the holes in the soles (but how was the water getting through those quart sized plastic bags I had donned over my socks?). Or maybe the slush was oozing in around the gaping tongue—I couldn't lace the boots because they really didn't fit my newly size Sasquatch feet (my shoe size changed during pregnancy). As I later discovered, the bags had slipped down and bunched up around my toes, and I didn't realize it because I had lost most of the sensation in my feet.

That afternoon, I spent naptime (what little nap overlap there was anyway) shoveling (while wearing sneakers) the remainder of the slush that had drizzled from the sky. I wished I could have taken a nap, too (because my back hurt and I had cramps), but I did not. I didn't want to have to shovel the next morning.

I had some time to think while I was out there. I realized I should count my blessings, rather than dwell on what was wrong. It was hard at first, but once I got going, it got easier.

Thank God I have a shovel (I saw our next-door neighbor

come back in his SUV with two new ones).

Thank God I have the strength to use it. (I wonder if I really should be using this time to work? No, I could work that night between Mark's ever-later bedtime and the one-and-only show I watched all week (which was on that night) and during Baby Chase's morning nap the next day (I knew he couldn't go to daycare since he'd had diarrhea after lunch, and the rule is, kids have to be bug free for 24 hours)...but...what if the daycare is closed because of the storm and Mark is home, too?).

Thank God I have work to do at *all* in this economy. I spent some time thinking about my writing project, and while usually I like to work in front of a computer, I knew I made some mental progress that wouldn't be too hard to transcribe.

I continued shoveling until I heard Baby Chase stirring on the monitor I'd brought outside with me. He had another big poop in his pants. I gave him a bath in the kitchen sink (I did not want to run the tub water because the bathroom was between the boybies' rooms and Mark was still sleeping) and then I worked on getting him to finish his nap. Shortly thereafter, I heard, "Mommy. Moooommmeeee. MOMMY! Hi Mommy. Mommmmmeeeeeee." Mark was ready to get up.

For the rest of Sunday until nunnight I was on Boyby Duty. I was able to work from 8:00 to 10:00, at which point I called it a night and indulged in my TV show, during which I fell asleep. I got up in a fog at some point when Baby Chase woke up crying.

On Monday morning, Baby Chase wouldn't nap. I was so frustrated because I had the deadline looming and I had counted on that time to work. And when we picked up Mark from daycare I noticed he was sounding increasingly raspy. "God," I prayed, "Even if he does get Baby's cold, please don't let him get the stomach bug thing…"

I worked during the afternoon naptime and I stayed up as late as I could, and then was up several times in the night with Baby Chase, who was still sick.

On Tuesday, we awoke to see that it had snowed again the night before and so I shoveled the driveway during Baby Chase's morning nap, and all the while misty precipitation hung in the air.

Mark's babysitter called me to come and get him after only two hours. (Fortunately Baby Chase was done sleeping—I learned early on, "never wake a sleeping baby"). He *really* sounded sick—"Hi Mommy, cough-cough-cough"—so I called our doctor's office yet again. After we finished talking about Mark, the nurse asked me how Baby Chase was doing.

When I told her that I had kept him home from daycare the day before because he was throwing up and pooping, and "generally kind of listless, certainly not quite himself yet," she said she was more concerned about *him* than Mark, so why don't I bring them both in.

I felt bad that I wasn't more alarmed than I had been over the weekend. "What kind of parent am I?" I wondered. But I didn't have time to entertain that thought—I had to get the boybies suited up and prepped for their doctor visit.

The soonest appointment we could get was early afternoon—right around naptime (which is probably why it was available)—so the boybies were just that much more grumpy. The doctor wanted to put Baby Chase on a new antibiotic, so I had to drag both cantankerous boybies to the pharmacy, where the service was awful, they didn't have the drug in stock, and it was $20 for the thing they *did* have (remind me again why I have insurance?).

In retrospect, I actually cannot believe how calm I was at the pharmacy with both boybies fussing, squirming, flailing, and generally creating a scene. And I wonder if people thought I was just used to all that chaos. The way they were staring, I felt like I might as well have had curlers and a hair net and a housedress on. With chipped nail polish even (if I wore polish these days no doubt it would be chipped).

In fact, while holding one boy in each arm and bounce-walking around the store while I waited for the pharmacy to fill the prescription, I ran into one of my former neighbors who said, "Boy, you really have your hands full." I was speechless. What is the right answer to that? (Maybe I *was* used to all that chaos.)

I didn't want to say—let alone even think—"what else could go wrong" because I sure didn't want to find out.

We got home, but Mark didn't want to nap. So I left him watching "The Diddy Show" (*The AristoCats*) because I really had to *try* to make some progress on the white paper—it was due the next day. Daddy was taking a redeye flight and would be home sometime in the middle of the night. He said he would be available to take Boyby Duty the next day so I could work, but I knew I would be even more exhausted by then and I cannot do good work when I am.

So, the next day, Wednesday, I spent 12 hours working. I had taken a brief shower and fixed food to eat in front of my computer, and once in a while I hung with Mark and Baby Chase at times when Daddy wanted to do something else. It was really awful trying to work when I could hear the boybies calling for me. I finally finished the white paper just before 7:00 p.m. and sent it off to the reviewer via email (he was in a different time zone, two hours earlier, so I made the "end-of-business" deadline). I remember sitting at my computer on the edge of my seat thinking (and probably saying out loud at that point), "C'mon, c'mon, tick tick tick…" because the graphics I had put in the paper made for slow going over my Neanderthal dial-up connection.

Thursday came and I was *so* ready for a break. The reviewer didn't owe me any comments until Friday's concall. I didn't want to think about work or the white paper (or anything) all day.

But, God answered my prayer regarding Mark and the stomach bug, and…

…*I* got sick. I realized mid-afternoon that I didn't feel so hot. I tried to be enthusiastic during dinner-bath-and-bedtime, but I could barely wait for Mark to go nunnight. I was in bed myself within 15 minutes, tossing and turning.

When I got up to feed Baby Chase at 3:00 a.m., I just couldn't get back to sleep. At 4:00 I got up and went and sat in the bathroom on the edge of the tub with my head in my hands waiting to throw up. I had reached the nadir of the week from hell.

I wish I could say that it ends there, but it doesn't. Obviously I lived to tell the story; I'll leave out the rest of the gory details. Suffice it to say that it took a few more days for the boybies and me to recover. They were both back to school the following Monday, and I'd produced the next draft of the white paper by then. Life went on. I was happy to leave that week in the past.

You must be a zombie

"You must be a zombie some days!" the newspaper editor said to me. I was talking about what it's like to work on a freelance basis rather than as a telecommuter who works during specific and predictable hours of the day for someone else.

"Yes, I suppose that's a good way to put it," I replied.

I thought about one day not long before when I was trying to put the finishing touches on a project outline for a new client. I was feeling overwhelmed because I wanted to impress this client, but I had been *flooded* with input and was having a challenging time sorting out what was the most important. I had been agonizing over it for a week and a half (during which time I had no daycare because it was the Christmas-New Year's double whammy, so that meant I have to work around the boybies' nap schedules, and if they don't sleep at the same time during the day—you guessed it—I work at night) and finally it had come down to the wire. It was due at noon that day.

The night before, after *finally* getting Mark to bed at 8:00, I had been working for nearly two hours when Baby Chase woke up hungry. I decided to go back to work after feeding him. At about 11:30, I realized I had reached the point of diminishing returns, and because I was also in the process of coming down with Baby Chase's cold, my head was all stuffed up and achy, and I was chilly. I decided to sleep in his room so we could both realize the benefits of the humidifier. (Plus I didn't want to bother Daddy with my sneezing, snorting, and coughing.)

Baby Chase woke up again at 2:00 and wanted to eat. Again. I shuffled downstairs to make another bottle and fed-rocked-burped and tucked him back in. Not much later I heard Mark's plaintive voice, "Mooooommmmmmmy. Mooommmmy!?"

I staggered into his room. He reached out, wrapped his arms around my neck, and clung to me as I bent over to peer into his crib. "Rock." "Milk." "Babar show." "Poopoo book." I capitulated on the first two requests, but no way were we going downstairs to watch videos or turning on any light to read *Everyone Poops.*

We sat in the rocking chair for a long time. Every so often I asked, "Marky, bed?" and he answered, "Uh uh." I tried to deposit him numerous times anyway, and each time brought forth a gale of tears. Now, I could have just left him, but my blood pressure tends to rise when my kids are crying, and I certainly didn't want to damage his little psyche...I want him to think bed is a nice, safe, good place to be. And I didn't want anyone else to wake up.

I was frustrated and annoyed—aside from tired—but I reminded myself that this was only one night out of many and he would not be small enough for me to hold on my lap forever, nor would he even want to be there! So, I made a bed for us on the floor with every possible blanket and pillow I could find in the room.

I tossed and turned and tried to avoid little feet kicking me—my back was still aching from carrying him half a mile after he fell at the playground a few days before, so the floor really was not the optimal place for me to sleep—and then morning came all too soon: it was just past 5:00 a.m. when Baby Chase called.

I didn't want to wake Mark up, so I crept out, made a bottle, and went back up to Baby Chase's room, which was where everything had begun at 2:00 a.m. Not much later, apparently sensing the absence of my warm body, Mark toddled in and joined us. We moved our party downstairs when the boybies got a little noisy so as not to wake Daddy.

The next two hours I spent gearing the boybies up to return to daycare after a week and a half off. Finally, at about 8:00 a.m., I sat down in front of my computer to write. I felt panicky. I had four hours to go before my deadline.

I decided to do a 20-minute stress-relief yoga video.

I sat down again and realized how tired I really was. I had a hard time focusing.

I drank coffee and drank some more until my hands were shaking.

All I wanted to do was sleep…and in fact, I sat there nodding from time to time, picking at my nails, chewing my lip—easily distracted—and I got up and paced a bit.

Finally I just sat down and wrote the outline. I pressed the send button at five minutes before my noon deadline. And indeed, that day I *was* a zombie.

Coffee juju

My coffee juju has gone bad. Both my coffee pot and go-cups seem to be jinxed.

We have this ultra-deluxe coffeemaker that we received as a Christmas gift. It was a timely acquisition, because our old Mr. Coffee had finally bitten the dust shortly after Thanksgiving. We were coveting the very model we were given, but bought a no-frills model for some ridiculously low-low price like $9.99 at our local Consumer Value Store (CVS) because we couldn't justify the expense of the one we *really* wanted.

But the ultra-deluxe model didn't seem to be the answer to all our prayers after all. Take today, for example. I had just barely recovered from cleaning up a coffee spill in my office—thanks, Teensy—that had gone all over my credenza (fortunately, there wasn't all that much in my cup—just the dregs of the first-of-the-day pot) and was looking forward to filling the cup back up with the pot I had put on to brew while I was in the kitchen rummaging around for cleaning supplies to attack the mess.

I walked back downstairs to find Daddy standing in front of the pantry closet eating corn chips out of the bag. His mouth was full, but he managed to grunt and gesticulate towards the corner. I was afraid to look. Had Teensy pooped on the rug to pay me back for tossing her off my desk the way I did when she knocked over my coffee cup? But no, it was our beloved ultra-deluxe coffeemaker, mocking me once again—coffee and grounds had erupted from the filter basket and were running down the counter onto the floor—

taking a detour into the drawers and cabinets—before splattering on the baseboard and wall.

"Do you want me to show you how ***I*** make coffee next time?" Daddy offered, always the gentleman.

I did not answer him. I seized the paper towels and got to work.

Just the day before, my go-cup had fallen on the floor and spewed its contents all over the white linoleum as well as the white legs of all four stools and the table. This is a new go cup—and doesn't automatically close. My old go-cup had a mechanism that when I pressed my thumb on a little lever, it opened the valve to let coffee pass, but the default position was closed.

But my old go-cup had met its demise not long before. Baby Chase had knocked it off the table and as it crashed to the floor, the lid popped off and broke into pieces. As luck would have it, I had just filled it, and that meant, not only the obvious—a full cup of coffee all over the floor—but also, the contents were hot. "Thank GOD, none of the coffee spilled on the baby," I thought, as I got down on hands and knees to clean up the mess.

With the new go-cup, I had to choose either open or closed and—my mistake—had left it open. It fell over when the "snack bag" I packed for our walk, which must have been top heavy, tipped over and bumped the cup, which rolled to the other side of the butcher-block island before falling to the floor. I watched in what seemed like slow motion while the coffee glug-glugged out—the lid had held fast—leaving a coffee trail in its wake before the big splash.

I had just freed Baby Chase from his high chair and of

course he wanted to see what all the fuss was about. I had to quarantine him in the family room behind the gate as I cleaned up this mess. He wailed in protest. My blood pressure rose as I crawled around on the kitchen floor under the table and between the stools, armed with baby wipes and paper towels, driven to my knees yet again.

Mark was alternately saying, "Baby be QUIET!" and "MOMMY LET'S GO!!! NOW!!!" Because both boybies were squawking, we departed sans coffee and I tossed some paper towels over the remainder of the spill to remind myself to finish cleaning the floor later. (As if I could ignore dark brown coffee on that white floor.)

This last episode is the crème de la crème of bad coffee juju. It was during dinnertime, a few days ago. It had been a long day—where it seemed like I was constantly cleaning up after the boybies. (I think I have permanent stains on my knees from kneeling in the midst of messes.) I was really looking forward to having a cup of coffee while we did bathtime and nunnight hour. I had teed up Ultra-Deluxe to brew, and turned my back on it while the boybies and I ate, as I always do. Given that these appliances are touted as "automatic," one takes for granted that they're going to do their thing without any user intervention.

We were almost done with our relatively messy dinner affair. Baby Chase is just beginning to use a spoon, and tends to fling more food than he gets into his mouth, but when he does, boy oh boy, is he proud of himself. And as I enthusiastically offered my what-seems-like 100th "Good job, Baby!" my thoughts turned to, "Boy, won't a fresh cup of coffee taste good just about now." When I looked over at Ultra-Deluxe, time stood still.

"Oh no." I said.

Mark added, "Mess."

I verified, "Yes. Big mess."

I liberated Mark from the dinner table and started over towards the coffeemaker to survey the damage. The mess required immediate attention, lest the walls become stained, was my assessment. In order to keep Baby Chase happy, I just kept offering him more and more food. He would be interested momentarily, but since he wasn't really hungry, he wound up conducting experiments such as

What will happen if I turn this bowl over?
What happens when I drop this on the floor?
Let's see what this feels like if I rub it on my head/in my ears/on my belly?
Does the diddy like cheese?
What will Mommy do if I keep beating my spoon on the tray?

I'll leave out the blow-by-blow details, but it took me 20 minutes to get this mess cleaned up. I started over, certain that the problem was that grounds were clogging the pause-and-serve mechanism, and since I had cleaned the entire device from stem to stern, it should be good to go. I started another pot and turned around to face the next mess on the agenda—The Baby. We went straight to bathtime, me without the benefit of my cup of coffee. It was brewing and I had tucked a dishcloth around the base of the coffeepot in order to thwart disaster, in case it was imminent.

When Daddy saw the dishtowel, and inferred what had happened, he told me, "You have to make sure you don't overfill the basket when you make coffee."

"Okay, honey," I said. But apparently I didn't learn my lesson, which brings us back to the beginning of this story. I had finished cleaning up the mess, but Daddy had disappeared. And I wanted a cup of coffee. My conundrum was should I wait for Daddy to demonstrate his superior methodology, or should I risk it—make my own pot—and stand by, just in case (since I just didn't trust Ultra-Deluxe).

Hmmmm. I wondered if all this is a sign from God to slow down and stop drinking so much coffee. But if I did, how would I get anything other than the bottom-of-Maslow's-hierarchy-of-needs action items accomplished?

Since both of the above choices required my standing around and watching coffee brew (and who has time for that?), I brought No-Frills out of retirement.

Expectations

"What did you expect it was going to be like when we had kids?" Daddy asked.

I sputtered a bit… "I don't know!" I wailed, deflated, and trudged off to tend to the current boyby "crisis."

But truthfully, back "then" (before kids), which seemed oh-so-long-ago, I am not sure I even expected anything specific. How could I know what to expect? There was no way I would have had any idea how it feels to be a mother. And even now that I am one, I can't always explain it. So how could anyone have explained it to me? It's one of those I-guess-you-have-to-be-there things.

How would I have known to expect that both boybies will be crying and I can't figure out what to do to make them happy and all I want to do is cry, too? And all of a sudden, they stop. They look at each other and smile and laugh—one minute misery and the next minute joy. In childhood, I suppose this is normal. In adulthood, it's usually classified as a psychological disorder.

How would I have known to expect that one boy will wake up from his nap right when the other one goes to sleep? Or the other one *finally* goes to sleep when it is time to get in the car and pick up the first one? Never mind that *I* need the nap, but rather than the nap I was going to try to get "one little thing" done. Or, I had given up on that one little thing because I realized I was too tired, decided to take a nap, and someone wakes up.

How would I have known to expect that sometimes when my fuse is short from being up for half the night and I feel like throwing things and screaming and being naughty right along with the boybies, one of them will smile at me? And how can I be annoyed then?

How would I have known to expect that when I am supposed to be stern and appropriately parental, I have a really hard time not laughing? Like when Mark thinks that just because he is being polite he can have whatever he asks for ... "Pease, Mommy. Chockit. Mouth, too." He's melted into tears a few times because I've told him we don't have chocolate for breakfast. It's so cute, I can't help but smile...but I can't let him see lest he think I am laughing at his misfortune.

How would I have known to expect that there are times when I am so exasperated I just want to get in the car and drive away. I think about packing and what I could fit in the car and how long I could be gone, and then my mind wanders to the diaper bag—is it stocked, how many outfits are in there, do I have the right size diapers, and what about bibs. And is there room in the trunk for two porta-cribs when the double stroller is in there...?

"Wait," I think. "That's exactly what I'm supposed to be escaping!"

And I realize I just can't. Nor do I *really* want to.

I have two kids under two. I guess I should expect...the unexpected.

The price of a shower

Someone sent me an email that contained this excerpt:

How to shower like a woman

1. Take off clothing and place in sectioned laundry hamper according to lights and darks.
2. Walk to bathroom wearing long dressing gown. If husband is seen along the way, cover up any exposed areas.
3. Look at womanly physique in the mirror. Make mental note: must do more sit-ups.
4. Get in shower. Use face cloth, arm cloth, leg cloth, long loofah, wide loofah, and pumice stone.
5. Wash hair once with cucumber and sage shampoo with 43 added vitamins.
6. Wash hair again to make sure it's clean.
7. Condition hair with grapefruit mint conditioner enhanced with natural avocado oil. Leave on hair for 15 minutes.

8 Wash face with crushed apricot facial scrub for 10 minutes until red.

9 Wash entire rest of body with ginger nut and jaffa cake body wash.

10. Rinse conditioner off hair.
11. Shave armpits and legs. Consider shaving bikini area but decide to get it waxed instead.
12. Scream loudly when husband flushes toilet and water pressure is lost.

13. Turn off shower.
14. Squeegee off all wet surfaces in shower. Spray mildew spots with Tilex.
15. Get out of shower. Dry with towel the size of a small country. Wrap hair in super-absorbent second towel.
16. Check entire body for the remotest sign of a zit. Tweeze hairs.
17. Return to bedroom wearing long dressing gown and towel on head.
18. Cover up any exposed areas and then sashay to bedroom to spend half an hour getting dressed.

This is in contrast to *How to shower like a man,* which includes far fewer steps, among them flexing in the mirror, tossing the towel on the floor somewhere, and waving "the winky" at "the wife."

Ha ha, right? But what about *How to shower like a mom with two babies?*

Because I am lucky if I can even take a shower! I consider it a bonus of I can. Very rarely am I able to shave my legs and wash my hair in the same session. And if I do wash my hair, I definitely don't "repeat" as the marketers of consumable products would like us all to do, and I certainly don't condition for even the one-minute recommended minimum.

These days, I often find myself accompanied by Mark (I can't let Baby Chase wander around while I am showering, especially if he and Mark were on the loose together, so usually I have to find the precise moment when Baby Chase is sleeping and Mark isn't bored enough to want to wake him up), who if he isn't peeking at me from behind the curtain, is doing something helpful and constructive (not) like handing me things off the counter or unrolling the toilet paper or dropping things (e.g., his toothbrush) in the toilet—a small price to pay for the luxury of cleanliness.

"At least he didn't flush it!" One of my friends consoled me. I failed to ask her what would have happened. I did learn, however, that it's pointless to try boiling a toothbrush to sanitize it—the bristles fall out.

But sometimes the price of a shower is just too high.

For example, last fall I was on the phone with my aunt talking about Thanksgiving and puttering around simultaneously. (I rarely have the luxury to *not* multitask—except while sleeping, but even then I could be doing something else, like nursing, or comforting Mark while "sleeping" on his bedroom floor.) I realized I had to go to the bathroom. Since I have a cordless phone, I went. Out of habit, I flushed, and then realized that while I doubt my aunt could hear me tinkling, the sound of the toilet flushing was surely a dead giveaway, so I had to 'fess up. "Sorry, I really had to go."

Well—what do you know—the toilet was clogged. And my first thought was, "What did Mark put in the toilet this morning?" (At that point he was about 21 months old.)

And then it started overflowing. Water wasn't just dribbling over the rim of the bowl…it was *cascading.*

I grabbed every single towel I could find (even the ones in the linen closet around the corner) as I told my aunt, "Oh, no—now I *really* have to go. Toilet. Overflowing! Bye!" And I pitched the phone out of the bathroom while she was winding down her end of the conversation.

Thankfully, I realized I could shut off the water at the base of the toilet. I cleaned up the mess and saw that I had generated a whole load of laundry.

In retrospect, I realized that Mark must have put at least half a roll of toilet paper in the bowl while I was in the shower. I had only just changed the roll that morning, and hadn't paid attention to its diminished status while I was on the phone with my aunt.

I wish I could say that the story ends there, but it does not. The next time I flushed the toilet, it overflowed again. And this time, since I had no towels handy, a torrent of water rushed out and found its way under the floor (there was no molding against the vanity, which is about 18 inches away from the toilet) and seeped through to the kitchen ceiling right above the area of the butcher block island where we took all but the most formal of our meals.

Until the time we moved out of that house, I was embarrassed about that water stain—the price I *continued to pay* for that one shower almost a year before (when I probably didn't even wash my hair *or* shave my legs)!

The emergency room

"Maybe *we* (meaning me) should see if he needs stitches," Daddy said regarding the gash over Mark's left eye. Not quite two, he had tripped over a giant stuffed toy crocodile and stumbled into the entertainment center. It didn't seem to be more than the typical fall-down-go-boom routine: Mark was crying, but he wasn't *too* broken up over it. So, we got out the fluorescent doobaids (bandages) and put one on him and one on Daddy. Mark wouldn't keep his on, nor would he tolerate an ice pack, so I had figured "Okay, it's naptime, anyway, let's just go nunnight."

Well, when he woke up, the cut was still oozing, or maybe he had brushed it with his sleeve…either way, this brings us to the big debate. Did he need stitches or not? I was hesitant, because I didn't think they would want to stitch a kid's face, and I figured butterfly patches would be tolerated about as well as the doobaids (I don't even know if they use butterfly patches anymore—I am referencing my own childhood, which was more than a generation ago, really).

Daddy said, "Well, wouldn't you feel bad if we (meaning me) found out he should have had stitches and he didn't?"

I weighed my choices and wondered what I would feel worse about, the potential scar or having to hold my child down while someone sewed his face up.

"Okay! Okay!" So I called our doctor's office. But since it was after hours on a Sunday, I spoke with an on call doctor that I didn't know. I felt so dorky trying to explain, "Well, he cut his head *several hours* ago, and I'm only just now calling…the cut's not too deep, but it's not really closing and kind of oozing."

The doctor suggested I take Mark to the emergency room. So, I got into gear and tried to get him psyched up to go in the *car.* To go for a ride with *Mommy!* Let's go get dressed—we're going to see the *doctor!* Fortunately, I had a diaper bag packed (I've learned) so we were out the door without much delay.

Well, it was a beautiful night with a full moon so we had plenty to talk about on the ride. "Dark. Stars. Moon. Horsey house. Cars. Night. Doctor!"

We got to the hospital, which is 25 minutes away. I wondered if I should have gone to the close hospital, but since it didn't seem like a huge emergency (I mean, we did wait several hours before *we* even called), we went to the bigger hospital. Our "regular" hospital, where all our doctors are affiliated and where the boybies were born .

I looked at Mark's cut again when we got out of the car. It really didn't look that bad to me.

When we checked in, the receptionist said, "Oh, no need to ask why *you're* here. Just have a seat; there are a few people before you. There are some toys in the corner under the TV."

I turned around and there were numerous other parties in the room. There were a couple of other little boys playing with the toys. I asked Mark, "Toys, Marky or sit with Mommy?" "Sit. Mommy," he said, but he wanted to watch the other boys. Their mother tried to rein them in, but I said, "That's okay, he's not sick or anything. He just might need stitches."

"Oh, I *see*," she said, eyes riveted to my son's facial wound. "I can't believe you're so calm."

Then I started feeling *really* guilty. What kind of mom was I that I didn't call the doctor right away, that I was hesitant about even calling several hours later, that I was "so calm!?"

And sitting near the TV was not the place to be. First of all, each of the three times our name was called, I didn't hear, and second of all, everyone was looking at us—or so it seemed. We were summoned twice before it was even time to go into the ER—once for admin and once for preliminary procedures, where the technician did a bunch of diagnostics and plastered some cold gel on a cotton ball to Mark's head and fastened it with a bandage. I prayed he'd keep it on because not only did it clean the cut, it supposedly numbed it. "In case he needed stitches," she whispered. I whispered back, "You don't have to whisper, he doesn't know what stitches are."

At last, our turn came to go behind the double doors, into the actual see-the-doctor section of the emergency room. The nurse technician wheeled in a TV/VCR combo with different selections that included Blues Clues. We watched an entire video while waiting for the doctor. Finally she arrived.

We exchanged pleasantries and as I was signing at the X's on the forms she had on her clipboards, the doctor said the nicest thing, "Well, I don't *have to* stitch it, but it would probably heal better." (Thank you, doctor!)

I turned around when Mark said tentatively, "Mommy?" and tried not to act alarmed. The nurse had swaddled him like an infant, arms bound to his sides.

I said, "It's okay, honey." (Though I really didn't think it was—I would have been freaked out to be mummified like that.) "Mommy's here." And I climbed up on the gurney with him.

I watched as the doctor stitched. I usually get grossed out by stuff like that, but I just imagined Daddy watching Baby Chase's birth by C-section and I figured if he could watch that, I could watch this. Plus, I didn't want to predispose Mark to the idea that anything unpleasant was going on. I had to put on a brave front.

He did okay until the fourth stitch and then started to lose it. Poor kid. It was late, he had been waiting at the hospital for more than two hours, and he was bound in a sheet, unable to move his arms and legs.

After the fifth stitch, the doctor proclaimed she was finished. I got off the table, the nurse unwrapped Mark and released him and he melted into my arms. We sat together for a few minutes to pull ourselves together. I was relieved that he had been such a good sport and that what could have been a miserable experience was actually not so bad (not that I'd want to repeat it any time soon…).

We were just gearing up to leave as the nurse came back to ready the room for the next patient.

"Ready to go, Marky?" I asked.

"I ready, Mommy!" Mark said. And to the nurse, "Thank you." and to all the other patients on the ward, "Bye-bye, nunnight!"

And we made our way back home, chatting companionably about "Dark. Stars. Moon. Horsey house. Cars. Night. Doctor."

Diet and exercise

After having two babies not quite 17 months apart, my body is in a state of disrepair. Besides being out of shape, two very energetic little boybies occupied much of my time and I often find myself "too busy" to eat right. And being hypoglycemic means that if I don't eat right, I eat very, very wrong!

If I forget to eat, my blood sugar level plummets, resulting in headaches and dizziness. When this happens, I crave sugar and other white food, which is usually categorized as "naughty" on any diet I've ever heard about. I try not to have cookies, chips, and such in the house, but if they happen to be here, they're not long for this world if I all of a sudden come up for air and realize I need to eat.

This probably explains in part why I haven't got my pre-pregnancy figure back yet. People are just so encouraging: "It took nine months to get that way, give yourself nine months to get back." Hello everyone, it's been eight months, and I still look four months pregnant (according to the post office clerk)!

Additionally, it has been hard to keep track of what and how much I actually eat. If I could remember what was in the empty plastic containers in the sink, I would know what I ate at my last meal (or last few meals, depending upon how long it's been since I emptied the sink). I've followed the Toddler Diet (cleaning off leftovers from Mark's plate), the Stand-and-Feed Smorgasbord (standing in front of the refrigerator while eating, no temperature modification or utensils involved), and the Double-Dinner Meal Plan (eat with kids and then eat again with Daddy). The point is, I haven't really been paying attention.

Furthermore, I think my metabolism has slowed down as a result of quitting smoking, which surely contributed to my impressive 50-pound first pregnancy weight gain that blossomed into a net gain of 80 pounds by the time I was ready to deliver Baby Chase.

Of course I know the formula for losing weight. Eat less and exercise more. Eating less would surely be easier if I slept more: not only would I have fewer available hours in a day in which to eat, but also, I wouldn't crave naughty food because I was overtired. (I don't believe there's a magic way to reduce by eliminating whole food groups or combining food synergistically.)

I recently decided to make a conscious effort to watch what I eat *and* to make a point of exercising regularly every morning. As I've heard one of my exercise gurus say, "the longer a woman waits to exercise the less likely she is to get around to it on any given day." That seems to be true in my experience.

I exercise at home, not because I don't want others to see me sweat, but because I can save time by not having to drive someplace, save laundry by not having to wear special clothes, and save even more time by not having to brush my teeth or perform other ablutions that usually precede leaving the house. I can even drink my morning coffee while working out, a practice that I am sure would be frowned upon in any gym. While I do remember hearing that Arnold used to drink beer during his workouts, that was back in the 1970s before we were enlightened. But the ultimate bottom-line key reason I exercise at home is—I don't need childcare.

And the fact that I don't have childcare is precisely why I use videos, and why it sometimes takes more than the allotted time slot to complete a video (but still less than if I went someplace else).

The following characterizes my typical exercise routine:

Baby Chase woke up early—it wasn't even 5:30—and I had stayed up way too late working the night before. So, I was groggy, but I figured, I might as well work out if only *one* of the kids is awake, especially this one. Mark likes to decree, "NO EXERCISING MOMMY—NO!" And he will purposely try to trip me up or jump on me while I am doing the floor work.

I put Baby Chase down and popped in a tape of my current favorite guy (who does abs in every workout) and went to get a cup of coffee. It was the previous night's old and yucky coffee, so I decided I better make a fresh pot. I had to start the tape over. It was one of the ones I recorded myself from the Health Network on cable, and there is no introduction—it launches right into the warmup.

Much of the routine was spent trying to avoid Baby Chase as he crawled around the room after me, wanting to practice pulling up. Another reason I exercise with this particular man these days is he has really simple and straightforward routines (rather than dance numbers taught by very coordinated women who were probably world-class gymnasts or aerobics champions prior to hosting their own shows).

Midway through the first segment, Baby Chase knocked my coffee cup over onto our beige carpet. I knew there was a break coming up—I'd done this tape enough to know the commercial I'd recorded along with the show by heart—so I ran to get paper towels and attacked the mess. Fortunately, no coffee got on Baby Chase (not that it was hot anyway), because this would have necessitated changing his clothes—he had school that day (it's one thing for *me* to go out of the house with coffee stains on my shirt, but what would people think if Baby Chase did?).

I had to rewind the tape again. Cleanup took us through commercial and beyond.

I attempted to do the sit-up segment twice, with Baby Chase lying across my chest for most of it. Halfway through the second time, Mark started calling for me. I didn't want Daddy to wake up, so I promptly stopped the tape again and went to get Mark. I told him, "Mommy needs to finish exercising, okay?" He said "Okay, Mommy!" I got him a juice cup, which kept him amused for most of the last segment of the tape before he started antagonizing his brother. I stopped the tape for the last time, doubtful that I'd resume it any time that day, but I'd just about made it to the end so we'd call it done. I consoled myself with the thought that I could always do some leg lifts while I was doing dishes or brushing my teeth.

My goal is to do this daily, even if it takes multiple attempts to get through one video, and even if said attempts are not concurrent. I owe it to myself and to my children to live and model a healthy lifestyle.

Freelancing isn't working

Working on a freelance basis means that I do not always have revenue-generating work to do during the hours that I have childcare. Freelancing is not the same as telecommuting, where you are on someone else's clock, which is typically during business hours. Or whenever it is, you can plan around it. People say, "Oh, aren't you lucky—you work at home." And yes, in some ways, I am. I don't have to commute (or even get out of my pajamas!) so I have a little extra time to do other things. Like housework.

But often I will be doing housework or errands during business hours—while I am paying for childcare—and then wind up working around the boybies' naps or when they're watching a show (unfortunately—I abhor having to use the TV as a babysitter), or attempting to work at unusual hours of the day—early morning or evening when I really should be sleeping.

Sometimes I wish I had the type of work where I could leave the house and go somewhere else to do it and leave it there when I came home. It's bad enough to have a boyby cry when I drop him off at daycare, but what's even worse is when I'm trying to work and I can hear him crying for me from the other room. Or if I am supposed to be working and he is in the *same* room, trying to get my attention and I am doing my best to ignore him. And the worst is the feeling of "Hurry up and go to sleep Baby, Mommy's client *finally* returned her call and now she has to deliver the goods."

Additionally, I don't have a lot of control over seasonal

fluctuations in work. One of my bread-and-butter projects is a quarterly magazine. That basically means for six to eight weeks I am working on this, then I have six to eight weeks off. The challenge I face is to find something to do during the six to eight weeks off. Looking for work while I'm doing work is nearly impossible (this is a trial for any self-employed person who wears all the hats), but waiting until I have the time to look for work, means, I am going to get the work right when the magazine project ramps up again, and then I will have *too much* work.

I had a slow period at the end of my pregnancy with Baby Chase, but there was no way was I going to go prospecting when I was eight months pregnant. I actually turned down a project because I didn't want to engage with a new client. No problem with my magazine project—I've been working with this client for four years and have an established relationship (i.e., have already proven myself). The kick off meeting for the fall issue happened when I was in the hospital delivering Baby Chase at the end of June—I had arranged to get my assignments early so I could get a jump-start.

At the daycare open house, other mothers with babies born in the summer were shocked that I'd be starting Baby Chase at the beginning of the fall term when he was just eight-weeks old. *They* were all waiting until October or November. It made me feel cold-hearted until I realized that a) I don't get paid if I don't work, b) he's only in daycare part-time and c) Mark has attended daycare for a whole year and I have every confidence in the place.

One day I overheard a conversation at daycare where so-and-so wouldn't be coming to school that day because his mommy took the day off to spend it with him. I thought to myself, "Gosh, if I had a day off, I would want to spend it alone." Immediately I felt guilty. What a horrible way to feel! Shouldn't I want to spend *more* time with the boybies? Shouldn't I be grateful that I have the kind of work I can do from home at any time during the day or night? Then I realized that working at "free moments" around the clock just isn't balanced and that the boundary between work and family is very blurry. Additionally, I am often thinking or worrying about "the next project." If I were on someone else's clock, I would know when the shift ended. But this way, I am always wondering if I should try to do that extra work…

I am certain that this kid-work-balance thing is something that mothers everywhere face. And for me, freelancing isn't working anymore.

Why Mark takes vitamins

I was talking to another mom a few weeks ago and asked her if her kids took vitamins. She looked at me askance and said that they didn't and that the pediatrician never said anything about *that* at their recent checkup.

I asked how the kids' eating habits were. She frowned a little, perplexed, as she said, "Okay."

I thought, "Really?" but I said, "Oh—you're so lucky!" Right, so now I'm going to a) admit that my older son's eating habits fall short of the USRDA for everything except sugar or b) call her a liar. Not.

Now that Mark is two it seems that he has stopped eating. He's a big talker when Grandma is over… chuckling over the names of exotic fruits and vegetables like Brussels sprouts, broccoli, rutabaga, persimmons…as *if*!

I tell him all the time, "Marky, eat up or pretty soon Baby Chase is going to be giving *you* hand-me-downs!" And I am not kidding—they are within two pounds of each other—and Baby Chase is wider. I'm guessing that in another six months or so they'll be the same size, which has totally thrown off my hand-me-down scheme. People ask me frequently if they're twins.

It only adds to my distress that in one of my parenting magazines this month, there were some sample menus that actually called for multiple ingredients. And cooking. Their suggestions included scrambled or hard boiled eggs, waffles, homemade vegetable soup, and steak teriyaki. (If I ever had time to cook anything like this, surely I'd end up eating it myself.)

Here's a typical day's worth of menus for Mark.

Breakfast

Offered: cereal bar, milk, and banana
Ate: apple juice

Snack

Offered: varies, provided by daycare or daycare parents
Ate: if it was "donut holes," he probably ate them

Lunch

Offered: cheese, crackers, applesauce, raisins, milk
Ate: not 100% sure, this was at daycare...only some of the crackers came back home. His "daily sheet" had the "ate some of my lunch" box checked off

Snack

Offered: homemade pudding pop with blueberries
Ate: chocolate chip cookie dough (while helping to make cookies for dessert), shared most of the pudding pop with Baby Chase, the rest was left to melt on the table

Dinner

Offered: pasta with tomato sauce and cheese, green beans, milk (would have had chocolate chip cookies for that night's dessert)
Ate: nothing. not hungry, probably ate too much chocolate chip cookie dough

Snack

Offered: vegetable fries, apple juice
Ate: two Chicklets (removed from mouth and stuck to duvet), cough drop, apple juice

So, that is why Mark takes vitamins!

The overdose

Baby Chase had been sick on and off for the past week. It didn't seem like the kind of sick where he needed to go to the doctor, but he was sick enough to wear me out. He had been throwing up every other day or so and he seemed to have acquired the sniffles on top of this. I had done countless loads of laundry and started on my second can of carpet cleaner.

I ran into the receptionist from our doctor's office at the drugstore when I was stocking up on sore throat pops, baby ibuprofen, and Blue's Clues toothpaste and she suggested if he didn't feel well the next day I should call. It would be Saturday, and she had the weekend shift.

Saturday night came and we had just made it through dinner hour, Mark not eating at all (as is typical), and Baby Chase making two attempts, which meant that I cleaned him, the tray, the chair, and the floor twice (before and after he hurled).

Baby Chase was being a nudge. He'd had a spectacular, fun day with Grandma (which is why I *didn't* call the doctor's office), and then a late nap...from which he woke up cranky. I figured he had a sore throat because every time he coughed or burped he would cry, and his cry sounded hoarse. Good thing I had the aforementioned ibuprofen and sore throat pops (but because he crawled around with the pops, I wound up washing most of them down the sink trying to keep them free from dust bunnies and carpet fuzz).

Mark was running around upstairs shrieking and Baby

Chase was in the bathtub and I was doling out the medicine. The dregs of the open bottle of ibuprofen were only enough for half a dose. So I opened the new bottle. Since I already had the minature-turkey-baster-plunger-thingy ready, I didn't bother to unwrap the new one. "Gee this bottle is awfully small, especially considering the size of the box," I thought.

I gave Baby Chase the other half teaspoonful…then I did a double take.

I looked at the bottle again. I noticed the word "concentrated" for the first time. I got that yucky adrenalin-rush-sick-to-my-stomach feeling. Time stood still…or so it seemed. People have said I'm a laid back parent, but this isn't the same as Baby Chase trying out Grandma's doggie's new rawhide bone or me scooping ice cream off the ground and putting it back in his cone. I had just O.D.ed the kid on ibuprofen!

Assorted rational and irrational thoughts flitted through my mind. "Well, it's only ibuprofen"… "It's not like the time my brother drank all the 'purple medicine' " (Dimetapp, back in the days before it was over-the-counter)… "I'm so careless!"…(Our mom gave him ipecac.) "I wish *I* had some ipecac" … "I'm a bad parent!" … "Just because it's an over-the-counter medicine does not mean you can't overdose on it" …(I remembered a kid in high school who had to go to rehab because he tried to commit suicide with Tylenol)… "Should I call the doctor?"… "What are the symptoms of ibuprofen overdose?" …"But…nothing bad ever happened to me when I took extra Advil…"

Baby Chase was in the bathtub complaining and I was trying to console him and to do the math in my head simultaneously. Mark was still running and shrieking. Baby Chase had half a dose, and then the half-teaspoon was really a little more than a dose by itself...well, how much more? This bottle says the full dose is for a 23 pounder, and Baby Chase weighs at least one third more than that...

I gave up trying to figure it out and decided I would give Baby Chase some milk to coat his stomach and slow down the absorption of the medicine...(and in the back of my mind I was thinking maybe the milk would make him hurl like it had just about every other night that week.).

Daddy got home and I 'fessed up. He said, "Well, how much more?" and I had to tell him I didn't really know. "No more than a double dose, I am sure of that." He said, "Well, I wouldn't worry about it...those drug companies are so conservative—you probably could quadruple dose him before you had to *really* worry."

I decided to call my mom after I put Baby Chase to bed. I left a rambling voicemail. Then I got out the calculator. She called back a short time later and said reassuringly, "I'm sure you didn't overdose him," and I said, "Well, I did, actually, but only an extra half-dose or so and he's sleeping like a log for the first time in a week, so maybe I should always consider giving him a dose and a half!" (Of course I had been in to check on him every 10 minutes since I put him to bed...because if you don't hear anything over the monitor, how do you know if it's really working?).

Apparently the ibuprofen wore off at 10:30 p.m. because it was then that Baby Chase woke up abruptly. We shared a restless night as I was reluctant to give him any more ibuprofen.

The next day, Sunday, I brought him to the doctor where we found out he had an ear infection. "No wonder," I thought to myself. (And I decided there was no need to mention my previous evening's faux pas.)

Housewife by default

I had approximately 20 hours a week of childcare coverage. In those 20 hours as well as whenever the boybies were sleeping (and I wasn't), I worked, and, since I worked at home, took care of the household, as well as the bulk of the other 148 hours a week of childcare.

One night it was 8:00 p.m. and I was supposed to be working on brochure copy, not only because I had just put Mark to bed, but also because I had needed a nap at 3:00 in the afternoon, so I had lost work time to make up for.

I didn't see how I would be able to keep up that schedule indefinitely and I often wondered about whether working was even worth it. Wasn't I working enough with all the other jobs I had to do? I realized I just might have to cut back on work…or even take time off. Gasp. What about my self-actualization needs?

I wrestled with this choice, but really there was no choice. (One's choices become limited when one has small children.) Daddy was certainly not going to stay home with our children. Daddy had a very demanding job. His previous job was similarly demanding, and so was the job before that. This meant he worked long hours. Furthermore, if he is not at work, he is working at home, or contemplating work, or recuperating from work, or looking for work.

Right around the time Mark was turning two my consulting work had slowed and the choice was made for me. I became more of a stay-at-home mom than a work-at-home mom. I reluctantly agreed to give up our beloved babysitter (who really was more like a second mom to Mark than anything else). I didn't completely give up daycare, but I did change the schedule: I had only two mornings of childcare a week, which was about eight hours.

How did this affect us? Aside from changing library day, I found myself often picking the kids up on the verge of late (jogging into the school, trying to look nonchalant) because I had attempted to squeeze in "just one more thing" during the morning. I was not as connected to the teachers since I didn't spend as much time lingering in the morning when I dropped off. In fact, I could hardly wait to get out of there. "Bye boybies, have a nice morning, Mommy will see you after lunch." "NUNNONONONO" Baby Chase would say, as I hand him to his teacher. And Mark, "No MOMMY! No school!" "Oh, but love, this is your *special time* with your friends and teachers!"

And besides having one less day of care, the two days I did have were Tuesday and Thursday rather than Monday, Wednesday, and Friday. This meant different friends, and different parents, too. Two of Mark's classmates moved up to the preschool room, and because of where his birthday falls, he "stayed back" in the toddler room. To add insult to injury, Mark's former babysitter's daughter started at our school that fall, and the only place he saw her anymore was on the playground—she was in the preschool room with his two friends.

It became essential to find some sort of structured (and inexpensive) activity for three mornings a week. I decided to try out our town's recreation department offerings. They had exercise classes in the mornings—and they offered babysitting for only $1.50 per kid! By actually leaving the house to exercise, no longer was exercising something that was fit in around other activities of the day, it had become a major activity, around which other things were built, such as trips to the supermarket, drugstore, post office, and bank, as well as cooking, cleaning, and all the other things mothers do that hold families together.

When I was in my twenties and focused on my career, I used to wonder what housewives did all day. I feel guilty for admitting that here and now, let alone even thinking it then. I feel like I owe all the stay-at-home moms out there an apology. I'm sorry. Now I know.

I just had to accept the fact that I must derive my self-esteem from other sources *besides* just a paying job. Nevertheless, I can't help but wonder what the combined value (in real dollars) of nanny, nurse, housekeeper, fiscal manager, social secretary—among others of the myriad roles I'd suddenly had to fill—would be.

Compliance insurance

"I'll give you *chocolate...*" immediately the sack of octopi I was carrying up the stairs for naptime quit thrashing.

"*Cho-o-o-o-o-ockit*," Mark repeated, his voice caressing the word.

"Yes," I replied. "As soon as you get in bed."

This was bribery, I know. But I was desperate to get the kid in bed for his nap. It was almost 3:00 in the afternoon and either he was going to bed right then, or he would skip his nap. If he went to bed any later, he'd be up all night, and if he skipped his nap, he would be grumpy and miserable until bedtime, and then probably be up all night anyway because his biorhythms would be out of whack.

So I put him in his crib and he said, "*Chockit*."

I said, "Yes, angel, let me get you organized...lie down, please."

And he was prone in seconds.

I tucked him in and he said, "*Chockit*."

I said, "Okay love, just a sec, Mommy has to open it." (Mark got chockit—er, chocolate—money in his Christmas stocking and it's in his top dresser drawer, getting doled out here and there. (In fact, I paid him one coin per hand the last time I cut his nails). "Here you go, honey. Nunnight, sweet dreams!"

"Nunnight, Mommy!"

For a long time, we needed a juicebox every time I picked him up from daycare or the babysitter's, or else he would pitch a fit about getting in the car seat. Rather than physically fold him in, I offered him a juicebox in exchange for his compliance. Now I offer the boybies drinks in order to keep their mouths busy because the ya ya chorus is getting louder and louder as time passes.

Gumballs play an important role in our lives these days, too. Mark learned how to chew gum right before he turned two. I chew a lot of gum—a habit left over from when I quit smoking. A couple of times I have handed over the quarter for Mark to get a giant, drool-inducing gumball on our way out of the supermarket. It doesn't take more than twice of any one thing for Mark to assume that is the way it will always be.

I was wondering how I would tell him no when the time came. But my dilemma was solved one day when I didn't have a quarter. I told him I was sorry. "Mommy doesn't have the money today. Another time. Next time. Let's go. Keep moving," I said as I dragged him to the car. He cried the whole way home and told Daddy on me.

One day, we went shopping to get a few last-minute things for Baby Chase's birthday, which was the next day. I made a big deal out of getting a quarter from Daddy, who kept spare change in his desk. "Now, hold on to it tightly, Marky..."(Daddy gave me a spare, just in case).

First we went to the drugstore, and I unloaded toys out of the cart as fast as he tossed them in. We got out of that store easy—with a 99-cent pack of pink Canada mints. These were my compliance insurance. Our friend, the store manager said, "Do you like those?" And Mark nodded affirmatively, "Yes. Do." And he does. He likes Altoids and grown up toothpaste, too.

As we were checking out (and I was separating the items that had mysteriously found their way into the cart from the things that I actually wanted to purchase), Mark was fixated on the "pops"—Tootsie pops and Blow pops, right there in front of him. The cashier was horrified by the tantrum that ensued when I told Mark we were *not* getting lollies, because we already had mints. The cashier might have been new, but he ought to get used to it if all that stuff is going to continue to be placed at kids' eye level. Retail marketing people do that no doubt hoping the parents are going to cave to avoid a scene.

Mark was more than mad at me as I hauled him into his car seat and he angrily threw the quarter he had been clutching the whole time we shopped. I couldn't find it in the car. "Thank God I have a spare," I thought.

But, then the scene in the supermarket (resulting from me vetoing most of his choices) was *so* awful—people throughout the entire store could hear him—that even though I had the extra quarter, there was no way I could let him get a gumball after his performance. It was a "major meltdown," as I overheard one fellow shopper say. I was holding him around his waist in a modified "poop carry" with my right arm as I fumbled to get my bank card out and complete the transaction with my left, all the while trying to appear blasé. ("Flailing little windbag? Where? I don't know anything about any flailing little windbag!")

As we passed the row of gumball machines, a fresh wave of tears and howled protestations erupted. I told Mark, "Naughty boys don't get gumballs." I felt bad because I am sure he didn't *want* to be naughty. He didn't even *mean* to be naughty. He just didn't have the tools to rationalize his impulses, especially when he needed a nap, which I'm sure he did. What had I been thinking, taking him shopping when he was tired?

The following Monday, when we went back to the supermarket to get everything we had to leave off the list that stormy day, Mark actually pushed his own cart (the child-sized one). I pushed Baby Chase in my cart. I must have been feeling brave to take them both in there, but Mark was a perfect gentleman...I think it helped that I weighed his cart down with two gallons of milk and all the frozen vegetables.

"What a difference a day makes," I was sure to comment out loud to our cashier and the store manager, who had both been there during our previous visit. And on the way out, we got the gumball—Mark's reward for his *good* behavior—a small premium to pay for compliance insurance.

Dusting the blinds

My mind wandered as I was preparing Baby Chase's birthday party invitations (a third of which were written out on random postcards that I dug up from the assortment of cards I keep on hand rather than buying another whole package of invitations—how things change from when Mark turned one).

I realized that I hadn't dusted the blinds in almost a whole year. I don't think. I may have dusted them at Thanksgiving (about seven months prior). Then again, I may have just turned them the other way (the way that I like better anyway, because they look more like shutters. They're wooden blinds.)

We have a lot of rustic wood accents in our house, and much of it is dark. In fact, the people who lived here before tried to lighten things up a bit in the kitchen, and painted over the dark wood trim, but it is determined to be seen, and the white paint has been steadily chipping off over the past two years. Having kids bump into it with walkers and toy trucks, and me with the Noo-noo doesn't help, of course. Then there are the slatted doors on all the closets upstairs, which are dust and baby powder magnets, as is the dark wood cabinetry in the bathroom.

I had to admit that things—not just the blinds (on both sides)—really needed a good spiffing up because company would be coming. But I just didn't seem to have the same motivation to clean that I used to. There is nothing like those last stages of pregnancy when the baby could come any day and I better do all those tasks I've been putting off or I'll just *never* have a chance to do them again. I was actually rearranging Daddy's bureau the day I was in labor with Baby Chase. No way would that task show up on my to-do list these days…actually, it wasn't on any list back then, either. It was totally spontaneous.

Somewhere along the line, most of my housework has become event-driven. That means that if there is no event, it doesn't really get done, except *maybe* on an ad hoc basis (like if I happen to have a paper towel and Windex in my hands, I might remember that the sliding glass door had some fingerprints on it last time I looked, and leverage my cleaning implements accordingly). Most of the time I used baby wipes to clean up messes. My how my cleanliness and orderliness standards had changed!

My how my *life* had changed…since Chase was born. I thought back to the beginning of Baby Chase's life. I was feeling all nostalgic about how things were a year ago. I was hugely pregnant. Anticipating. And Mark was my only child. I couldn't imagine what life would be like with another baby, and now I couldn't imagine what life would be like without him.

Everyone said the first year with two babies so close together would be really hard, which it was. But now that the year has flown by, they have begun playing together more and more. I am fully convinced that God made Baby Chase robust so he would catch up to and keep up with Mark. Oftentimes, because Baby Chase stretches and Mark regresses, they are on the same wavelength.

Baby Chase is somewhat wary about attempting to stand up or take steps in front of Mark, and in fact often either crouches or toddles over to something he can hold on to while he waits for the whirlwind to pass. And I don't want to hurry him, either. Once he starts walking, we won't be able to call him "Baby Chase" anymore. And I couldn't imagine what life would be like when both boybies were going in different directions.

I remembered a conversation I'd had with Mark's babysitter about six months before. I had said, "I can hardly wait until Baby Chase is old enough to play with Mark."

She said, "I know, it must be so hard when they are both so young but both at different stages."

(I think she was worried about me. She had given me a stress-relief yoga video and a relaxation audiotape that she made for Christmas.)

I answered, "Yes. Well…what was really hard was the first three months…"

I don't have any idea how I would have managed if it weren't for the help I got from family, friends, people at church…and especially one of my best friends who came over several afternoons a week. Just having her here to hold Baby Chase helped me to feel like I was an individual person again, separate from him.

And Baby Chase really did need to be held a lot. Not that I minded holding him, but he was such a huge baby that it could be exhausting. I had tried a sling and a baby carrier with Mark and we hadn't gotten the hang of it. The thought did little more than cross my mind with Baby Chase—too hot and too big. He outgrew his infant car seat with the carrying handle by the time he was three months old. That meant I had to carry him in and out of stores or wherever until he was strong enough to sit up in the shopping cart. I hauled him around slung over my shoulder like a sack of potatoes a lot.

Then when Baby Chase was three months old, there started to be some regularity to his behavior. When he turned six months, then he could sit by himself or go in his walker or the bouncy thing in the doorway, which would free up my hands for…

"Kids grow up so fast," Mark's babysitter had said, interrupting my reverie. I was holding Mark during this whole conversation and he was clutching his Amy.

I had replied, "Yeah, one day they're not going to want to sit on our laps anymore."

She'd added, "They won't want to have anything to do with us. They'll come home and go straight to their rooms and shut the door."

I sighed, shook my head to shut out that thought, and continued writing the invitations.

(And sometime during the week prior to Baby Chase's party, I did wind up dusting dust the blinds, as well as performing a bunch of other spot-cleaning feats.)

Doing the next right thing

"I want Mommmmeeeee!" Mark wailed. I tried to peel him off of me to hand to Daddy, but every time I dislodged one of his little hands from my hair, necklace, or blouse, it would clamp back on when I went to work on the other one.

Baby Chase—who was one year old that day—was at my feet saying "Mommmommmommmommmaaa!" with increasing urgency, as he picked up on the desperation in his brother's voice.

I was going on a job interview.

The downturn in the technology industry had made it harder and harder for me to find projects. When the magazine I wrote for regularly ceased publication altogether, it was as if I had been laid off—without the ability to collect unemployment benefits. I had to replace my income...but I hadn't yet figured out how.

I had weighed several options—and even tried some of them—while trying to figure out that next right thing. Should I try to find—and then perform—more writing work (which, in truth, had become increasingly difficult over the past year since Baby Chase was born)? Should I look for a full-time job with full-time childcare? Or perhaps a full-time night-and-weekend job with some childcare? (Though my friends who do "split-shift parenting" have told me it puts a major strain on their marriage as they are rarely able to spend any time all together.) Or should we try to make it on Daddy's income while I take on the role of full-time homemaker? Except at that time, Daddy was out of work. Again.

As a working mother, I don't think I am ever going to be in balance except for the merest fraction of an instant. Like the economic theory that says the market always strives towards equilibrium (where supply and demand intersect), which is a point constantly in flux—just like my life. I constantly strive for balance, and then something happens and I get thrown off, and then I strive again, simply continuing to make corrections to my course by doing the next right thing. I'll do what I have to do in order to best take care of my children, even though the decision is sometimes painful and the consequences are not always desirable.

When Daddy finally separated Mark from me, and I gently shook my leg free of Baby Chase, I said with as much cheer as I could muster, "Goodbye, my angels. Mommy loves you." And then ducked hastily out the door so no one would see the tears in my eyes. My heart was breaking for my sons since I knew that the anguish they were feeling was very real to them; at their tender ages, they did not yet have the tools to overcome emotion with logic.

This particular job opportunity practically dropped on my lap: I mentioned my predicament to my sister-in-law and it turned out that she knew someone who went to school with someone who was married to someone who needed someone. It was a part-time professional position, which, as I had come to realize through my investigations, was very scarce, especially considering the current economic slowdown. I just had to check it out.

As I drove to the office building, thoughts of the one hour each way commute (no more 30-second commute from kitchen to office, often without getting dressed, or even brushing my teeth, never mind putting on makeup), the additional childcare I would need to find (there is a considerable lag time between demand and supply for this requirement) were interspersed with "children have to learn to deal with disappointment sometime, right?" and "They can't always have things their way." These latter thoughts buoyed me up. Because while this job wasn't the scenario I had originally envisioned as I imagined my life as a working mother, I knew I couldn't always have things *my* way either.

"Why would you want this job?" the hiring manager queried. "With your qualifications, you could find a full-time job earning more than twice the salary we're offering."

Though I had not rehearsed a politically correct HR-approved answer, the words flowed from my mouth: "At this point in my life I am not interested in climbing the corporate ladder and shattering the glass ceiling. I just want to be able to earn a living and be there for my children as much as I can be. I no longer derive all my self-esteem from my job, nor do I define myself with my professional status."

Furthermore (but I kept this part to myself), my choices are not as broad as they had been before I had children, and this job—while not my dream job—had the potential to be a pretty good fit.

After just days of negotiating, I was offered the position.

I thought about how wonderful it had been to be home with my babies for their first years, even though the boundary between work and family was sometimes fuzzy. I figured that with this new scenario, this "next right thing"—I would realize better quality time for both professional *and* personal pursuits. I justified that taking a job outside the house just made sense by proving a theory I once heard: that working mothers can have it all—just not all at once.

And so I accepted.

Thank you, God

One time when Mark was 15 months old, he followed me up the stairs and I didn't know it. When I reached the top landing, I turned around and there he was, halfway up, just standing there, not holding on to anything. All I could envision was him falling down backwards and…choking off a gasp, I turned around and headed back down, sauntering casually past him. I let out my breath slowly as I got right behind him to escort him up safely. Thank you, God.

One time when Baby Chase was five months old and he was in his walker, he discovered the ficus plant. I had to extract a whole bunch of leaves from his mouth. I thought those were poisonous, but apparently not. Thank you, God.

Then there was that time I was bustling around the kitchen. All of a sudden I realized Mark was quiet. Too quiet. I looked over. He was contemplating a knife, both hands around the handle, point up. Not a butter knife, but one of the ones from the butcher block. I realized then that he could reach the dish drainer. I grabbed for it. My mistake. A tug of war ensued. Fortunately, I ended up with the knife and neither one of us was stabbed. Thank you, God.

Right after Baby Chase started walking he pitched forward towards the bathtub where Mark was enjoying his baff. I couldn't catch him and cringed as his face broke his fall. I was so sure he broke his nose. Then I saw that all the blood was coming out of his mouth. I ran cold water on a washcloth and tried to clean him up and calm him down. He was screaming and trying to catch his breath—choking not only on his sobs but also the blood in his mouth. Of course this freaked Mark out and he started crying, too. He then got out of the tub and nearly bowled Baby Chase and me over—I was kneeling on the floor holding Baby Chase—as he wrestled and nestled his way into my lap. Never mind drying off. At the same time I was trying to keep Baby Chase's face turned away from Mark so he wouldn't see the blood. It was only when Baby Chase took his bottle and was able to drink from it that I figured he didn't need to go to the emergency room. Thank you, God.

There were numerous other events that have caused me to thank God, including tricycle wipeouts from which Mark emerged unscraped as well as running and tripping while carrying magic markers that resulted in a colored forehead (as opposed to a poked out eye). I am sure that as time passes, Baby Chase will be plenty more in need of God's watchful eyes, as he is so intrepid as to inspire the nickname "SuperBaby," bestowed upon him by the lifeguard at our town beach for his fearless sand and water and antics as well as his ambassadorship to all strange animals that wander onto the beach.

But this episode takes the cake. We were at a 4th of July party and it had been a very long, exciting day culminating in skydivers jumping into the backyard of this party and Mark only had a short car nap on the way back from activity #1, lunch at Grammie and Papa's country club where he went swimming for the very first time in his life, which in itself, must have taken a huge amount of mental, never mind physical, energy.

He wanted to go home, so he headed down the driveway. I was trying to say goodbye to the hostess and other guests, and he said "Mommy, come *on*!" for the second or third time, and I guess he didn't believe me when I said I was coming. He just took off.

The car was almost at the end of a long downhill driveway that let out onto a street with no sidewalk, so there was no distinct barrier where the driveway ends and the street begins. Mark and I have an ongoing battle with parking lots and walking in public in general, as he rarely wants to hold my hand or even the stroller. He says, "no, WALK!" as if walking and holding my hand (or the stroller) are mutually exclusive. I could hear cars whizzing by, but in retrospect, I realized those cars were driving on the major route that goes parallel to the road the party was on.

This all happened so fast. I called, "Marky." "MARK." "MARK!" Then "Stop! No!" as I was speedwalking, then running, then all out flying down the driveway, having flung all the bags I was schlepping. I was sure he would stop at our car, but he didn't. And then I knew he was in God's hands because there was no way I would catch him by the time he reached the street.

And then he just stopped at the end of the driveway. I was upon him in an instant.

I swooped him up and hugged him to me so tightly—maybe too tightly—and tried not to smile (which sometimes happens when I am nervous) because this was serious. He said, "Ha ha, funny!"

And I said, "NO! IT ISN'T! IT'S NEVER FUNNY WHEN YOU RUN AWAY FROM MOMMY!"

"Why, Mommy?"

"Street. Cars. Danger!" "Mommy was *scared!* It's NOT funny!"

"I'm sorry, Mommy."

"Please, Marky. Don't *do* things like that!"

I was holding him all this time and he wanted to be set free, but I would not let him go. We waited for Daddy to come with the keys. I made sure I told Daddy the story in front of Mark, just as I reiterate stories where I am proud of him.

Later on, we were lying on the floor together playing with his trains. He said. "Mommy sad. Mark run away. Street. Cars fast."

"That's right, Marky." I said. "Mommy sad. Mommy scared. Mommy angry. Danger!"

"Why, Mommy?"

"Because cars go fast in the street. What do you think would happen if you ran out into the street and a car was coming? Or what if a car was coming into the driveway?

"Car bump Mark."

"Yes, honey, car bump you, and it could hurt you! It could break you. And then Mommy would be so sad. Mommy loves you so much, Marky. Mommy doesn't want you to get hurt. Mommy doesn't want you to get broken. Ever!"

"Here you go, Mommy. Thomas Engine. Your turn!"

"Thank you, Marky."

Thank you, God.

Thank you, God, for entrusting to me these adorable and wonderful, lovey little boybies! Please help me remember what a blessing my children are even when they do really naughty things like banging on the screens and throwing toys, singing the "ya ya song" louder and louder in the back-seat of the car even after I have asked them to stop repeatedly, digging out the entire tube of ChapStick and wiping it I-don't-know-where-and-don't-look-forward-to-finding-out, waking up much earlier from their naps than I expected, as well as when they throw their dinner on the floor, pour water out of the tub and onto the bathroom floor, refuse to go to bed, and especially when they get me up for the day at 4:00 a.m. Please help me to be patient and stay sane. In the name of Jesus Christ, Amen.

When the "next right thing"...isn't

I was talking with my new "boss" on the phone one morning, firming things up for my impending start date the following day. We were finalizing logistics and a red flag went up. It had been my understanding that the job had some flexibility in days, and perhaps in hours, too. And that not far down the road, after a relationship had been established, I could do the work at home.

But it turned out that the boss man wanted me there in the office on a day when I had not arranged for childcare. It turned out he expected me to take a lunch break (I told him I usually work through lunch, eating at my desk). So this would mean I had to arrange for an extra half hour of childcare every day, *including* the day that I still had "uncovered." (It irked me enough that I'd need childcare for two hours a day while I was commuting!)

What it all boiled down to was that this was more of a "do-the-time" type of job (as opposed to "get-the-work-done")—the lunch-break thing cemented this fact for me. After I subtracted my childcare costs from the pay, I would be making $25 a day, which works out to one-third of what my 15-year-old stepson, who was living with us at that time, earned after a day at his landscaping job. That is before taxes, and before wear and tear on the car. And that didn't take into account that I would be imposing on family for extra childcare and support for as many as 15 hours a week, never mind the fact that I'd have to get dressed up.

To top all of this off, Baby Chase was sick (which meant he couldn't go to daycare and I didn't have a contingency plan to cover such an occurrence—aside from staying home with him.). I had slept in his room with him the night before and was up numerous times, each time as I lay back down in bed I wondered, "What have I gotten myself into?"

I reflected on how I had been scurrying around for the past month, trying get all my ducks lined up in a row, *as though I had been told I only had four weeks left to live.* That feeling was looming large in the back of my consciousness, but I was trying not to think about it. I certainly couldn't bring myself to say it out loud to anyone, even myself.

Then I thought about how that day would be my last day of "freedom" with the boybies…the last day that I'd have the option of lingering at daycare during drop off…the last day I could run back over if I forgot something important (like leaving the car seats for a field trip)…the last day I would be available to turn around on the way home because Mark forgot Toby the Tram Engine in his cubby. There would be no more playdate on Monday afternoon or Library Day on Tuesday or beach day on Thursday. No more afternoon walks…whenever.

What my gut was telling me was that what I *thought* was the next right thing was truly not right at all. The reality was that I would be working a part-time job that somehow was starting to take up way too much of my time and energy. As my mom said, "Listen to your intuition. This whole thing is going to take more out of you than it will give back. Good for you for being willing. Good for you for reconsidering."

Then came the time when I had to explain my decision to both the recruiter and the boss. I don't think there is any way he will ever understand—he has no children. And even if he did, his wife would be the one in my shoes, not him. I had left them both messages (which included telling them my son was sick), they had left me messages in return (neither mentioned my sick son) and now in everyone's favorite game of Phone Tag, I was "It."

I put a picture of me and the boybies—the one that I was planning to bring to work for my desk, ironically—in front of me as I made the calls.

The recruiter told me she was disappointed, but I know she understood. She told me that many women with two kids in daycare know that they're just going to break even. They take a job as an entrée back into the business world (I did not bother to remind her that I am not planning to reenter the business world as most people know it, and in fact, the thought occurred to me that it is now time to take all my suits to a consignment shop). I just said, "I'm really sorry, it's just too much to ask of my family to pick up the slack. It's better to know now than in three weeks."

To the boss, I said, as I started trying to explain the economics of it, "Well, I am sure you don't need to know the nitty-gritty details, especially since we're just not on the same wavelength given the fact that you don't have kids..."

"But I do have nieces and nephews," he offered, sounding slightly miffed.

(But you were never one with another tiny being, and you never gave up a part of yourself—that is now walking around in someone else's little body—as that one became two).

"...I just won't ever be able to make this job my #1 priority." (For example, right now I am physically and emotionally exhausted from being up all night with a crying baby and would rather take a nap than work).

We parted on cordial terms. I am sure one and perhaps now two of the other people I referred to the recruiter will get jobs with this company, so everything will work out.

(To their credit, both the recruiter and the boss man did ask me about Baby Chase.)

And even though I felt absolutely spent and more than anything in the world wanted to take that nap, I felt incredibly light and completely free...which is kind of amusing, considering I am at the beck and call of two small tyrants, one of whom woke up from *his* nap (thereby robbing me of mine) just as soon as I hung up the phone with Boss Man.

Yet, with my newfound knowledge, I went in to greet Baby Chase with more gratitude and appreciation than most days when my best-laid plans have gone awry.

The natural mother onus

"She's a natural mother."

I find that so insulting. Because not only is the pressure on, but also it implies that it's easy to be a mother…or it should be anyway. What a lofty image to live up to!

No one is a *natural* mother; we all have to learn. But when I'd hear that term, I felt that if it didn't come naturally, something is wrong with me. Perhaps a lot of things would come more naturally, if I could just stop second-guessing myself. I was often plagued by uncertainty thanks to the ever-changing rules of the AAP and all of the advice of our well-meaning and "expert" friends and relatives—and sometimes even complete strangers.

For me, becoming a mom was a shock. Changing from a career-minded person—who had almost a decade and a half in the work force post-college, and whose pre-college work experience had nothing at all do to with children—into a mother was trial by fire.

Am I not supposed to think being a mother is hard? Because I do. And I also have a hard time admitting that I think it's hard. And it's hard to face the fact that I can't just do everything I want to do anymore. Of course, when I had kids, my wants became a lot different than they used to be. In fact they melded with my needs: eating and sleeping and bathing.

I got so tired of talking about vanilla things like nap schedules, play dates, the latest recalls, and "has he said 'da da' yet?" I have found that most people will not freely admit how hard it is to have children, to try to balance family time and work time and the ever-elusive personal time, to function effectively in a state of chronic sleep-deprivation, or to parent, co-parent, and maybe step-parent too. How does everyone else shoulder all their difficulties? Is it not difficult for them? Or perhaps they are speaking in some politically correct code that I have yet to decipher fully.

As time passed, I became more confident that I couldn't possibly be unique in my challenges. And in fact, my suspicion was confirmed at a 4H Fair, where I spotted another mom who had two children, almost the exact ages as mine. Since we had this obvious common bond, I initiated conversation. I asked her how she was doing and she said something to the effect of, "I am tired of pretending it's not hard."

Be still, my heart! "So am I!" I said, and as-meaningful-a-conversation-as-possible-with-four-kids-ages-two-and-under-at-a-fair-after-ice-cream-and-before-naptime ensued. Bottom line: we agreed that it was definitely hard, but definitely worth it.

For me, the transformation into and within motherhood—my mothermorphosis—was abrupt. It was hard. It was unfathomable. And it will no doubt continue to evolve outside the capacity and scope of my imagination. It was *not* natural.

My heroines

"Would you like some help?" another mom asked as I lumbered out to the daycare parking lot, six or so months pregnant, carrying Mark, his car seat, and a variety of accessories from the morning.

I used to pride myself on being self-sufficient, but have come to realize "What's the point? Why not accept help?" Especially with a baby, and being obviously pregnant.

So, I said "Yes, thank you…can you take the baby for a minute?"

And she said, "If he'll come to me." And he did. (He must have recognized an experienced mom.)

I was fumbling around trying to get the car seat back into the car and was making conversation. "How many children do you have?" I asked, knowing that she wasn't the mom of anyone in the infant room where Mark goes. I figured she might have a toddler, maybe two.

She said, "I have one in the preschool room and four humminahumminahummina." This is what I heard, anyway, because I had my head and part of my body in the back of the car.

"Excuse me?" I said, withdrawing my hulking frame from the car and giving her my full and rapt attention.

She repeated, "My three-year old goes here and I have ten-month-old quadruplets at home."

I was amazed and incredulous. I said, "You must be the person I read about in the newspaper … you moved here to be closer to your family …" I felt like genuflecting. Here she was, a mother of *five* boys and she looked so with-it, so put-together, and she was offering to help *me*—disheveled and fumbling pregnant mother of *one*.

I vowed then and there that if I ever caught myself complaining, I would think about her. Or any of my other heroines, like "The Twins' Mom" (she delivered her second set of twins when the first set was barely two) and people who have kids even closer in age than mine like a few moms I know whose kids are just over a year apart, or a friend at church who has five kids, the oldest of which was in kindergarten at the time, and none of them are twins.

One time at a church potluck supper, I thought I was clever to ask my mom to help me divide and conquer because I did not think I could manage my two boybies by myself. But then I saw my friend walk in with her brood. She was there with *all* of them. And they were the nicest, most well-behaved kids—Mark and I were playing with three of them in the nursery after dinner. They all got up and went running when Mommy called them to go home, unlike Mark, who I had to drag kicking and screaming, even though I had given him the two-minute warning.

As time went by, however, I realized that comparing myself to other people only served to make me feel incompetent and inept. And putting other people on a pedestal doesn't do them any favors either. We're all just doing the best we can. I might not be able to do what so-and-so could do—or *appeared* to be able to. And then I found out that "appeared" really is the key word. What's easy—or looks easy—for one person might not really be. My church friend later confirmed this fact by telling me that sometimes she feels harried on the inside even when it looks like she has it all together on the outside.

I no longer intend to be shy about receiving or offering help. I think we need all the encouragement and support we can get.

My hopes for my sons

In my hospital room, later in the day on which Mark was born, a nurse was showing me how do to basic newborn things: breastfeed, burp, change a diaper, and "cord care" (for some reason that term always tickled me).

Mark had that very solemn, watchful, and silent newborn expression on his face, including knitted brows. The nurse commented on how serious "the little guy" looked. My immediate response was, "Ohmigosh, I *know*...I hope he's not always like this! I hope he lightens up!"

Duh. The kid is 12 hours old and I'm already panicking about his personality? (Little did I know at the time that probably all newborns spend some time in that serious, watchful state—at least mine did.)

Weeks later, when I was writing in the "notes from Mom" section of Mark's baby book, I had a moment of clarity.

I realized that no matter who Mark turns out to be, I hope and pray that he is the person that God wants him to be, and that he's a happy and productive member of society. (And I wish the same for Chase and now Griffin.)

One time when Mark was two and half or so, he was fooling around with the buttons on my clock radio and he came across one of my favorite Lynyrd Skynyrd songs, "Simple Man." I used to just like the tune, but now that I'm a mother of sons, the words took on new meaning. I stood Mark up on the bed and we slow-danced while I alternately hummed and sang the chorus:

"Boy, don't you worry... you'll find yourself.
Follow you heart and nothing else.
And you can do this if you try.
All I want for you my son,
Is to be satisfied."

Sometimes I see the boybies doing something that I think is particularly skillful or clever, which may or may not be just one of those things little kids do: coloring, dancing, singing, grooving, banging—and I imagine they will be the next Picasso, Gregory Hines, Steven Tyler, or Bob the Builder. The possibilities are limitless.

I can encourage them and nurture them and socialize them and care for them and teach them and love them—but ultimately I know that who my sons become is not entirely really up to me. Because, as the song says, "don't forget son, there is someone up above."

Visit www.MotherMorphosis.com

Mom-Writers PUBLISHING COOPERATIVE

We empower mom writers.

Publishing the Works of Extraordinary Mom Writers

Wyatt-MacKenzie Publishing, Inc

WyMacPublishing.com